Praise for
The Last Addiction

"There is a different life beyond addiction. Read this brilliantly crafted, true book. Then read it again. There's hope in these pages. A new life, a better life. Take it."

> —GREGORY L. JANTZ, PhD, C.E.D.S., founder
> of The Center for Counseling and Health Resources Inc.
> (www.aplaceofhope.com) and author of sixteen books

"Sharon Hersh is a brilliant artist of the heart whose broken story radiates with the mystery of relentless, down-and-dirty, truth-filled love. It is scandalous to claim, as Sharon does, that an addiction bears a gift for the addict and for all those who care for him. If it is true—and it is—then shame is not our final covering, nor is sorrow our only friend. If you know you struggle with gods that are not your creator but have created madness, loneliness, and heartache, then the journey of *The Last Addiction* will bring you face to face with the One whose transforming love is our deepest desire."

> —DAN B. ALLENDER, PhD, president and professor
> of counseling at Mars Hill Graduate School, author
> of *Leading with a Limp* and *To Be Told*

"A must-read for anyone who wants to go beyond addiction into the heart and soul of recovery."

> —WILLIAM COPE MOYERS, author of *Broken: My Story*
> *of Addiction and Redemption*

"I love this book because Sharon reveals the most beautiful truth: We're all addicts. And we all have Hope."

> —PETER HIETT, pastor and author

THE
LAST
ADDICTION

THE
LAST
ADDICTION
WHY SELF HELP IS NOT ENOUGH

own your DESIRE

live beyond RECOVERY

find lasting FREEDOM

SHARON A. HERSH
MA, LPC

WATERBROOK
PRESS

THE LAST ADDICTION
PUBLISHED BY WATERBROOK PRESS
12265 Oracle Boulevard, Suite 200
Colorado Springs, Colorado 80921
A division of Random House Inc.

ISBN 978-0-87788-203-9

Copyright © 2008 by Sharon A. Hersh

Published in association with the literary agency of Alive Communications Inc., 7680 Goddard Street, Suite 200, Colorado Springs, CO 80920, www.alivecommunications.com.

Library of Congress Cataloging-in-Publication Data
Hersh, Sharon A.
　The last addiction : own your desire, live beyond recovery, find lasting freedom / Sharon A. Hersh. — 1st ed.
　　p. cm.
　ISBN 978-0-87788-203-9
　1. Compulsive behavior—Religious aspects—Christianity. 2. Addicts—Religious life. 3. Substance abuse—Religious aspects—Christianity. 4. Redemption—Christianity. 5. Love—Religious aspects—Christianity. 6. Liberty—Religious aspects—Christianity. I. Title.
　BV4598.7.H47 2008
　248.8'629—dc22
　　　　　　　　　　　　　　2007041710

Printed in the United States of America
2008—First Edition

10 9 8 7 6 5 4 3 2 1

SPECIAL SALES
Most WaterBrook Multnomah books are available in special quantity discounts when purchased in bulk by corporations, organizations, and special interest groups. Custom imprinting or excerpting can also be done to fit special needs. For information, please e-mail SpecialMarkets@WaterBrookPress.com or call 1-800-603-7051.

To all who want...More

CONTENTS

Introduction

THE GIFTS OF ADDICTION

Without suffering, happiness cannot be understood.
The ideal passes through suffering like gold through fire.
—FYODOR DOSTOEVSKY, *The Brothers Karamazov*

We are living in a time when the books about people's private lives are flying off the shelves, stories of unthinkable shame and pain as well as stories of exhilarating overcoming. We thirst for memoirs that tell us that, even though our own lives might not be as crazy as the ones we are reading about, we can find our way out of the mixed-up mazes we are lost in. We gulp down stories of men and women who have overcome difficult childhoods and lonely journeys through private hells—sometimes of their own making and sometimes of the making of others—in hope that we too will be overcomers. We are drunk with stories about alcoholics, drug addicts, overeaters, sex addicts, gamblers, bulimics, and people who love too much.

And we are hung over. Sometimes our heads hurt from the aftermath of reading stories that turn out to be untrue. More often, our thinking is blurred by stories that don't parallel our own closely enough to sustain our hope. And many stories leave our throats parched, thirsty for more, even n they are true and close to home, because we can't find the key to open our own door to join the overcomers.

This is a book about addiction, which is both the motivation and the cause of our quest. Every addiction confines and crushes the human spirit with cruel and unusual punishment. I know. My own drinking began as a prescription from a doctor for anxiety and ended in some unthinkable places that deeply hurt me and those I love. I will tell you more about my own experience with addiction throughout this book. But this is not a book only for alcoholics or drug addicts or those who love them.

I hope to stretch your thinking about addiction. The truth is that no one escapes the reality of compulsion. Everyone loves something too much. Everyone struggles with passion gone awry. That's why we're all buying all those books. If you believe you don't struggle with addiction, you're probably more addicted than I am. In his wonderful book *Addiction and Grace,* Gerald May wrote, "It is as if these severely addicted people have played out, on an extreme scale, a drama that all human beings experience more subtly and more covertly."[1] We all suffer from the same condition. We all seek a resting place from striving and suffering, and we often cling to what promises to be a haven, only to find out that we have created our own hell. I hope this book will deepen your compassion and commitment to yourself and to others, all those who are in bondage to something that initially promised to make everything better, until it made everything worse.

This book looks at the hard realities and possible redemption within substance abuse, but addiction reaches much further:

- the good church woman whose eyes are lined with fatigue and whose heart is filled with frenzy, but still she cannot say no
- the man who spends hours a day on the Internet, jeopardizing job and family life

- the person who has no sense of individual self and is consumed by striving to become who, what, and where everyone else needs him to be
- the woman with the flawless makeup and wardrobe who does not know how to face her obsession with appearance or where to confess the toll that it is taking on her own soul
- the man or woman who longs for a real relationship, yet spends every night and weekend in front of the television, watching unreal stories
- the man who cannot keep up financially because he has gambled away everything he makes—and more—on Internet gambling sites
- the woman who ingests thirty-two laxatives a day and engages in the unspeakable ritual of binging and purging to maintain her weight
- the man or woman who strays from marriage in serial affairs, whether they are physical or emotional in nature

Part I begins by uncovering the lies we tell about addiction. We will look unflinchingly at the evidence, the energy, and the experience of addiction. I hope this book will help you *tell your own story.* Telling our own stories requires that we recognize addiction for what it is. As we see more clearly our own hearts and our longings for intimacy, we will be able to put words to the lengths we will go to kill, satisfy, control, or find substitutes for those longings.

Part II tells some true stories about addiction. But I warn you, not every story concludes with the happy ending that is common in popular memoirs. Writing something that will sell often produces a highly edited version of oneself or the subtly embellished version. In truth, we learn most about ourselves and the true meaning of redemption in reading of strugglers who fall down, get back up again, and fall down again.

Yes, this book is about redemption, in every chapter—what it looks like, how it is experienced, and by whom. In Part III we will consider what redemption looks like, not only for people who know that they are addicts, but also for family members who watch in anger and agony as their loved ones relapse time and time again. This is not a self-help book. I am deliberately not using the words *recovery* or *overcoming*, because these words can get us into more trouble. That's the last addiction, the idea that I can save myself with myself. We know—I mean deep down *we know*—that it is futile to try to save ourselves with the very selves that got us into trouble in the first place.

In the final chapters of this book we will examine the healing path and what it means to live—really live—in newness of life, free from self-defeating, self-enslaving patterns of behavior. I think that's what we all want—a fresh start, a way to begin again, a new chance. This book does not conclude with a list of things to do to get that fresh start. Instead, it closes in an encounter with a Person who asks the question: What if—*what if*—we are in a dance of intimacy with ourselves, others, and God, a dance that heightens and unfolds through all the phases and seasons of our lives, even in the dark days of addiction, and this dance is the journey of redemption? That would mean that intimacy, connection, and belonging are not just the destination of the healing path, but that relationships themselves are the path.

To see relationships *as* the healing path may seem unlikely when we have been hurt, abandoned, and betrayed by relationships, but they can be redeemed. To *redeem* means to "buy back." I believe Love is waiting to buy back all that has been lost, abandoned, or violated and to give us a certain fullness in this life. Relationships with self, others, and God are intended to be our resting place, our balm for suffering, our place of confession, our tastes of heaven here on earth. We get in trouble with addiction when we find substitutes for healthy relationships and require them to be our all, right here, right now. Redemption comes at the point of no return (which is why it most often happens in addiction), because we have nothing to return to. Our substitutes for healthy relationships have betrayed us. We've sold our souls to something or someone false. But what if there is another character in this story, a Love that redeems us? What if Love becomes the one Reward of our hearts and lives, allowing us to give and receive more fully in all our relationships?

How can I write, "Love redeems us"? Those who have experienced addiction personally or within their families know that love is shot to pieces by addiction. In my own life and the lives of countless people I have seen in my counseling office, I have witnessed the sobering reality that addiction is stronger than human love. Powerful natural disasters like hurricanes or tornadoes do not compel fathers and mothers to abandon their children. But addiction does. How many times have I heard from anguished and confused family members, "Why couldn't he wait until after my birthday to get drunk?" Or, "How could she go back to the same thing after all the money we've spent on treatment?" I have heard, and said myself, the self-loathing words of the addict, "Why do I do the same thing over and over again?" Or, "What is wrong with me?"

In his compelling autobiography, *Broken*, William Cope Moyers described the excruciating reality of self-contempt for addicts and their families:

> My father was sitting in the front passenger seat. Turning around to look at me, he saw a thirty-five-year-old crack addict who hadn't shaved, showered, or eaten in four days. A man who walked out on his wife and two young children and ditched his promising career at CNN. A broken shell of a man, a pale shadow of the human being he had raised to be honest, loving, responsible. His firstborn son…

"There's nothing more I can do," he said. "I'm finished."

All these years later, he tells me that's where the conversation ended. But whether I imagined it or not, I heard him say something else.

"I hate you."

And I remember looking in his eyes and speaking my deepest truth.

"I hate me, too."[2]

Just last month I heard a similar story of hopeless self-defeat. I sat in my office across from a thirty-eight-year-old man who wanted to quit drinking. He smelled of the beer he'd drunk just before coming to see me. His hands were shaking from his attempt to withdraw from his twenty-four-beer-a-night habit. Tears streamed down his face as he described the train wreck of his life. He'd lost his job, his hobbies, and his relationships. He couldn't get into an inpatient treatment facility for at least five days. He'd been attending Alcoholics Anonymous meetings at the urging of his mother, but he needed to drink just to sit through a meeting.

I imagined his mother sitting in her home in Texas, willing the telephone to ring with the news that he had made it to the treatment facility. She was willing to pay the nearly thirty thousand dollars that the treatment would cost. She needed to believe that it would "work."

I was slow to make any promises to this man. First of all, I knew that his brain was pretty hazy with alcohol and he couldn't hear much that I had to say. Second, I have watched many family members and clients climb on the roller coaster of treatment. I myself have been in detox, inpatient and outpatient treatment, ninety Alcoholics Anonymous meetings in ninety days, and deliverance prayer meetings. I have taken antidepressants, Antabuse (a preventative medication that makes you physically ill if you ingest any alcohol), and vitamins. I even endured ten days of IV drip treatment intended to "rebalance" my brain with nutrients and amino acids. *All* of these treatments have been part of the redemptive process in my life. *None* of them has been the single answer.

I decided to wait, to not tell this man yet about Love's redemption in the midst of addiction. I knew that he had a ways to go before he would even care about redemption. Right now, he just wanted to stop feeling like he was crawling out of his skin.

The truth is that he never called me back. I don't know whether he ever made it to treatment or not. I still think about his mother. But I will not join those who say in disgust, "Addicts! There's just no hope. They are like a dog that goes back to his vomit." Instead, I pray for my one-visit client to stay in the journey of addiction and redemption, even though it often looks like taking one step forward and two steps back. I know that if he hangs in there, he will experience the gifts of addiction.

You read that right. I am convinced that the experience of addiction and redemption can include many gifts. This book considers the gift of getting caught, because this is when we have the chance to experience being known, loved, and still wanted. We will find the gift of wisdom in telling the truth about addiction and its place in our lives. We will examine the gift of humiliation that leads to the gift of surrender—the ability to exchange my way and will for another Way and Another's will. We will look at the unlikely gift of woundedness, because wounds, no matter how painful or unsightly, are where Love gets in with the healing gifts of mercy and forgiveness. And all along the way we will be looking for the gift of hope. Hope is what pulls the soul forward, and if you are mired down in an addiction or love someone who is addicted, you know that hope can become a scarce commodity. Finally, we will define the gift of freedom, that newness of life that doesn't mean the ability to do whatever we want, but that releases in us a longing to want the One in whom we were created to live and move and have our very being.[3]

It doesn't take too many years of doing the two-steps-forward, three-steps-back dance of addiction to know that we can't give all of these gifts to ourselves. The great gift of addiction is that sooner or later it proves to us that we are not gods.[4] There we come face to face with the last addiction. We realize we are our own worst enemies. We're enslaved by the last addiction—our own determination to repress our destructive desires, our own ability to keep the rules or do the steps, our own religious zeal to rein ourselves in, and our own decisions to chart a different course. In our last stand, we are addicted to our own will, our own self, our own ability, our own pursuit of control.

This great, unspeakable gift of addiction has been to teach me that *I cannot set myself free. I must be set free.* This book, however, does not advocate a complete abdication of human choice and effort. Nor does it advocate a passive spirituality. Learning what I am responsible for and what God is responsible for is key in the journey of addiction and redemption. The question of responsibility raises the question of who God really is. God is Love, the most powerful force in the universe. Love alone can free the human heart. Love is where our hope lies. Throughout this book, I will share my own meager understanding of Love through story—my own stories and the stories of others. Even so, an intellectual understanding of Love will not deliver us from addiction. We need *more.* The New Testament describes the power of Love: "It's the only way to shut down [the] debilitating self…"[5] This same book of Scripture equates God and Love and reassures us that "God is greater than our worried hearts and knows more about us than we do ourselves."[6]

In other words, Love is the opposite of fear. Beneath every addiction, in the addict or the addict's family, there is a deep reservoir of fear—fear of relapse, judgment, consequences, the inability to change, stigma, misunderstanding, and defeat. When you are afraid, you *can't* experience Love. The apostle John wrote, "There is no fear in love. But perfect love drives out fear, because fear has to do with punishment. The one who fears is not made perfect in love" (1 John 4:18, NIV). Love is our way out of fear and our Source of redemption. Most of us have tried many things in our search for Love, desperate to find something that outlasts our bad choices and that undoes human failings. I want to tell you that for all your life, Love has been looking for you. I hope, through the stories of other addicts and their family members in this book, you will open your own heart to Love. If you do, you will begin to hear, not in human words, but in spirit, "No matter what you have done or others have done to you, I love you for your own sake."

I suspect that reading this book will bring up many emotions for you: fear, cynicism, anger, sadness, and hope. I know that when we have been hurt or hurt others, opening ourselves up to Love is the most frightening thing there is. But paradoxically, when we open ourselves up to Love, fear begins to be dismantled. Before reading further, consider saying out loud or to yourself, "I am willing to want Love."

Centuries ago, the mystic Julian of Norwich wrote about her own experience of opening herself up to Love:

And so by meekness which we obtain in seeing our sin, faithfully recognizing his everlasting love,...our love will never be divided in two.... If there be any such liver on earth, who is continually protected from falling, I do not know, for it was not revealed to me. But this was revealed, that in falling and in rising we are always preciously protected in one love.

If this approach seems a bit esoteric or suspect to you, I encourage you to take a chance and read on. The process of acknowledging the lies we tell about addiction, considering the true stories of addiction, and beginning to see the truth about redemption can open us further to Love.

Perhaps this openness to something Other than ourselves is the greatest gift of addiction. Our self-will might be able to force us to change for a time, but when we realize our need for redemption in addiction, we have to acknowledge that self-will is not enough. Only Love can move us to change every day, one day at a time. Whenever I hear stories about self-will run riot and self-effort falling flat on its face, I have an opportunity to consider what (or who) plucked me from that fate. I do reverence to Love every day.

PART I

THE LIES WE TELL
ABOUT ADDICTION

Whatever we are ultimately
concerned with is god for us.

—PAUL TILLICH, *Systematic Theology*

1

THE EVIDENCE OF ADDICTION:
A MILLION LITTLE PIECES

> Sharing the personal story of what happened in the
> addiction, what brought the person to change,
> and what life is like in recovery…is a ritual that
> enables the holy presence to come forth.
> —LINDA SCHIERSE LEONARD, *Witness to the Fire*[1]

I know a sixteen-year-old boy who shoots heroin between his toes twice
a day because that's the only place left on his body with a good vein.

I counsel a thirty-two-year-old woman who ingests twenty-eight laxatives a day and spends hours in an unspeakable ritual of binging and purging to satiate her hunger and maintain her weight.

According to the January 7, 2004, *Fond Du Lac (WI) Reporter,* Timothy Dumouchel of West Bend has filed a claim against Charter Communications blaming the company for his "TV addiction" and claiming that "TV…caused his wife to be overweight and his kids to be lazy." He is suing for five thousand dollars, or three computers plus a lifetime supply of free Internet services.[2]

Years ago I attended church with a woman who read her Bible for thirty minutes every day because she was afraid of what God would do to her children if she didn't.

One of my first clients in my counseling practice was a hard-working man who made eight hundred dollars a week and spent half of it on telephone calls to 900 numbers talking about sex to women he didn't know.

The authors of the *Diagnostic and Statistical Manual of Mental Disorders* are considering adding "text messaging addiction" as a diagnosable mental disorder.

As we begin to consider addiction and the infinite number of ways that compulsion and obsession become entwined in the human condition, I open this chapter with the story of a few addicts I know—a few stories that may or may not be familiar to you—to confirm the words of the Old Testament prophet Isaiah, "Their land is full of idols" (Isaiah 2:8, NIV). After all, that's what addiction really is—it is worship. No matter how sophisticated or crude, any given addiction is a person, place, substance, activity, or ideology that becomes central to a human being's mind, body, soul, and spirit. Whether it is alcohol or religious activity, addiction is at work when something or someone begins to affect the style and nature of all aspects of a person's life and interacts with all of his or her activities. The etymology of the word gives insight into its idolatrous nature. Addiction is from the Latin word *addictus,* which means "to surrender to the gods."

THE MOMENTUM OF ADDICTION

Addiction is in motion when a person, place, substance, activity, or ideology becomes what you think about when you wake up in the morning, what you plan for, what you hide from others, what you spend money on, what causes guilt and/or shame, what you spend time trying to mitigate, and what you determine to eradicate, only to find yourself in the same cycle again. Your addiction becomes the momentum of your life. It is the most significant relationship in your life. Often, not until you make a decision to change a central activity or relationship do you realize the momentum it has acquired. From a physics perspective, changing momentum is about as difficult as making a river flow upstream.

Addicts are people who are living, sometimes obliviously and sometimes quite consciously, with the consequences and ramifications of their one central activity. Addiction is the cumulative impact of many long-cultivated and interrelated habits of mind, soul, and body. Much of the literature about addiction defines it as "a state of compulsion and

> Humpty Dumpty sat on the wall.
> Humpty Dumpty had a great fall.
>
> —Nursery rhyme

obsession, focusing on one element that will supposedly satisfy." This definition is incomplete, however, because it leaves out the heart of addiction. Addiction goes deeper than obsession and compulsion. It is worship. It is giving my heart and soul over to something that I believe will ease my pain and provide an outlet for my fury at being out of control in a world that hurts me, scares me, or leaves me alone.

Addiction creates a way of life—a way of being in this life—that is fueled by a deep, deep need to worship something or someone. As the songwriter suggests, "You're gonna have to serve somebody."[3] The addict bows at the altar of a central activity that takes away stress, pain, and loneliness for a while *and* gives him or her a sense of control. All addictions include a re-creation of a more palatable world. In addiction, we believe that our chosen idol creates a world that is better. All of us long to re-create. The soul longs for rest—relaxing, letting down, having someone else do the work. Like a magic carpet, our addictions allow us to dissociate from reality and connect us to a god that seems to work much better than any god we may have learned about in Sunday school.

ADDICTION MAKES EVERYTHING BETTER
UNTIL IT MAKES EVERYTHING WORSE

This book is not a statistical manual about the prevalence of addiction in our culture. I suspect you have already felt its impact. In fact, the moment we record statistics about addiction, they change, usually demonstrating an increasing impact on society. Perhaps the most significant statistic is summarized by Robert R. Perkinson in his comprehensive report on drug and alcohol addiction in 2004; he concluded "that there is not a family in America that has not been impacted by addiction."[4] Addiction has left countless individuals and families broken into a million little pieces.

Rather than report statistics that are impersonal and make addiction seem far away, let me tell you one woman's story of addiction and her search for redemption. Her story is not the stereotypical tale of a drunk living in a shelter, sipping cheap booze from a bottle in a paper sack. This woman's story is lived out in the suburbs while she sips chardonnay from a plastic Big Gulp cup.

When Laurie came to see me for counseling, she was in her late thirties. She was well dressed and articulate, wore designer shoes, and had on flawless lipstick. She began by telling me, with great shame, that she had a little problem with alcohol. She was married, had two children

> And all the king's horses and all the king's men couldn't put Humpty together again.
>
> —NURSERY RHYME

and many friends, and was active in her church. No one really knew about the alcohol. Laurie was concerned though, because she had begun to notice that the amount she was drinking had increased. She occasionally felt shaky in the morning, and she had even been drinking during the day recently. Most often, however, she waited until after dinner, poured herself a glass of wine, and sipped it while watching television or reading, until she fell asleep.

Concerned about the increasing amount she was drinking, Laurie had consulted her family doctor. She was worried that she had begun to drink more than a "little" wine each night, felt guilty about the habit, and worried about health risks that she might be incurring. Laurie's doctor suggested that she begin to take Antabuse, which would stop her drinking, so she could then more clearly evaluate the impact it was having on her life. Laurie looked up Alcoholics Anonymous on the Internet and attended a few meetings on the other side of town. A few of the people who spoke during the meetings seemed strongly opposed to taking any type of medication. One man had made fun of therapists.

As Laurie's inability to quit drinking on her own became more clear and her desperation for a change in her life increased, she contacted a local outpatient treatment program by telephone. As is often the case with substance abusers, Laurie could not articulate the specific damage that her daily drinking was doing in her life, but she lived with a sense of unease that things were not as they should be. The outpatient treatment counselor suggested that Laurie come in for treatment, which would last a hundred days. She would attend three-hour meetings three times a week, and the cost would be over three thousand dollars. Because Laurie's insurance would not pay for treatment, she faced a dilemma common to addicts: Is the cost really worth it? Is my problem really that bad?

Laurie also courageously disclosed her concerns to the pastor of her church. He suggested that she attend church more regularly and wondered if she was really serious about her faith.

She did see one therapist who was on her insurance. He told her that Antabuse could really damage her liver. He didn't think that Alcoholics Anonymous worked and suggested that they do weekly therapy. He wanted to start by talking about her relationship with her father.

Laurie saw another counselor who was more spiritual in her approach. She told Laurie that if she really understood herself and God's love for her, she wouldn't want to drink. Laurie really liked this therapist but continued to drink the whole time that she saw her.

Laurie's story reflects the reality in many addicts' lives and the lives of their families. From the outside, her life doesn't look out of control. Does she really have a problem? Laurie's story also reveals that identifying the true nature of the problem is complicated, and coming up with a solution seems almost impossible. It's almost easier to diagnose the problem and solution for the homeless woman on the corner with the brown paper bag and the sign that says "I need a miracle. Please help me."

Near the end of our consultation, I simply said, "You must feel so confused and alone in all of this."

Laurie's true agony and the growing destructive momentum of her life are revealed in the words she choked out: "I know I have a problem with alcohol. I fill up a large plastic glass every night with wine. Every night I drink wine, and sometimes I feel hung over in the morning. I'm participating in a Bible study on breaking free, and it has made me realize I have a problem, but I don't want to bring this up at the Bible study. I'm sure no one there would understand. My husband drinks a lot too. He sometimes thinks it's a problem and sometime doesn't. Actually, the alcohol helps my marriage at times, because it loosens things up sexually. I wonder if I could just stop drinking, except for when we want to be sexually intimate. Oh, I don't know; it all sounds so stupid. And I feel guilty all of the time."

Every sentence in Laurie's declaration betrays the grip that this addiction has on her heart and soul. Laurie believes she has found something that relieves the pain and stress of life and allows her to re-create her world for a few hours every day. I understand Laurie's attachment to her nightly glass of wine. During my own drinking days, whenever I would hear of a friend or family member who was suffering illness, financial ruin, or any kind of distress, I would think, *If only you knew my secret friend (alcohol). It makes everything better for a time.*

I wanted to respond to Laurie with compassion and respect. She deserved both. Her secret distress and her unsatisfying attempts at finding help revealed a woman desperate to drink and desperate to stop. I knew

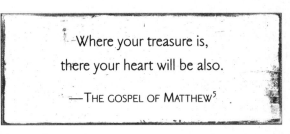

> Where your treasure is,
> there your heart will be also.
>
> —The gospel of Matthew[5]

that she was caught, caught in the trap of addiction. On one hand, she wanted deepened passion for herself, her family, and her faith, and on the other hand, she wanted to spend all her passion in the predictable ritual of worship with her nightly Big Gulp cup of wine.

Picking Up the Pieces

I knew that for Laurie to find redemption, she needed to see more clearly the evidence of her addiction.

So far, all attempts to stop had only left her confused about her problem and its solution. Together we set out on a course to examine her life and look at the evidence. For every addict, four pieces of evidence are always present. These are four proofs or signs that addiction is at work. The evidence is revealed in four conclusions that addicts come to about themselves in the midst of the momentum of an addiction: I am Crazy, I am Alone, I am Unforgivable, and I am Hopeless. All four conclusions are not always present at the same time, but each will surface at some time during the addictive process.

In the rest of this chapter, we are going to look at these four conclusions, as well as begin to ask the questions that might lead us or our loved ones out of the rubble of addiction. It is important to note that these four pieces of evidence don't apply just to substance abuse. They are present in the life of anyone who is worshiping at the altar of a god that promises relief and a sense of control, only to deliver more pain and chaos. One of my students who was not a substance abuser describes his own answer to the question, "Am I an addict?" As you read his words about his addiction, you will see traces of his fear of his own craziness, his belief that he is all alone in his struggle, his fear that he is unforgivable, and his ultimate conclusion that he is hopeless:

> I heard the stories of an alcoholic drinking and then vowing to
> never drink and pouring the liquor down the drain. And I thought
> of myself, young and scared, in my family room, looking at images
> [on the computer] late at night and then quickly deleting it all,
> clean up the computer, leave no trace, and VOW, "Never again!
> That's it, never again." I heard about the drug addicts who would
> be so high they would have to drink to go to sleep, and I thought
> of myself struggling and fighting to resist. Don't do it, you don't
> want to, but I do, no you don't, yes I do, but you shouldn't, but I
> want to.… I would fight in my mind for hours, lying awake, unable
> to sleep. Finally, just look, get it over with, you can't win anyway.…
> And then the tears. I remembered when the tears stopped. I remem-
> ber when I stopped fighting. I remember when I stopped caring. I
> remember when I stopped asking for forgiveness. I remember when
> I just gave in. And that is why I am really an addict.

I AM CRAZY

Craziness is best defined as "a commitment to a person, place, thing, or ide-ology that makes our lives unmanageable." The stories of craziness in addiction are at times so extreme as to be nearly unbelievable. I worked with one woman who was obsessed with her pastor. She came to see me for counseling after she was caught climbing over the ceiling tiles in her church to eavesdrop on her pastor as she crouched above his office. I might have thought that she was certifiably crazy and referred her to the local psychiatric hospital if I hadn't known my own craziness. In the midst of my own addiction, I would often determine that I was not going to drink. I would throw out my bottle, sometimes with alcohol still in it, and firmly plant the trash cans at the curb, willing the garbage collectors to take away my love-hate relationship with Smirnoff's 80-proof vodka when they took away the trash the next morning. More times than not, however, I would creep out to the curb in the wee hours of the morning, crouch down behind the trash cans, and swig the rest of the alcohol, drinking straight from the bottle.

The question to ask when you hear or experience stories of addicted craziness is, what do you understand of desire? Why would an otherwise sane person get trapped in a momentum that renders his or her life unmanageable? The answer is desire. Desire is intended to be the fuel of human relationships. It propels us to want to engage with others and with God. God made us to hunger for relationships. Addicts are ensnared when they believe that they can completely and continually satisfy that hunger with something that ultimately devours them.

The New Testament explains how desire can open the door to crazy behavior. The apostle Paul writes, "[God] puts a little of heaven in our hearts so that we'll never settle for less." God created us to want belonging, security, peace, beauty, acceptance, rest…*more.* And yet the reality is that we are in a "stopover in an unfurnished shack, and we're tired of it!"[6] Addicts experience a taste of heaven—in a Death by Chocolate dessert, exciting sexual intimacy, a new outfit purchased at the mall, or a five-thousand-dollar bonus for a month of hard work. Then we want heaven on earth all the time, and we become willing to go to crazy lengths to obtain it. Simply put, addiction arises when we turn something good into something bad. We eat a dozen doughnuts at one sitting, binge on pornography on the Internet, max out our credit cards, and work ourselves to the point of exhaustion. These are a few crazy behaviors fueled by desire. Addicts find that their longings for mutual, satisfying relationships are often disappointing, complicated, and out of their control, so they substitute a quick fix of something that seems more predictable and in their control.

Do you hear the craziness in Laurie's story? There's something about a suburban, middle-class soccer mom drinking an entire Big Gulp cup of wine every night that might make us smile. Or cry. Especially when you hear the desire in Laurie's story. Her desire for connection with her children, for passion with her husband, for transparency with her Bible study, for self-respect for herself—these desires are all thwarted by the consuming relationship that Laurie is in with alcohol. Laurie's addiction is a perfect example of desire gone awry. And although her craziness may not seem extreme, the cry of Laurie's heart is excruciating: "Why do I keep doing what I don't want to do and can't seem to do what I really want to do?" Hers is the true cry of an addict.

> Our problem with desire is that we want too little.
>
> —C. S. Lewis, *The Weight of Glory*

One reason that we attach our desire to addictions is that all desire risks disappointment or even agony. All desire can open the door to loneliness and shame. There is no person who can fill all of our emptiness. Even the best marriage or the healthiest friendship fails us at times. When we have been disappointed or shamed, we come to believe that the way to escape loneliness and shame is to rid ourselves of desire for relationships. Addiction is an attempt to escape sorrow and remake my world so that my desires are satisfied. When all I want is a bag of potato chips and a Blockbuster movie at the end of the day, I don't have to live in the tension of desire for anything more.

I Am Alone

The evidence of crazy, unthinkable behaviors in our lives makes us afraid: I am alone. We often joke in AA meetings that only alcoholics believe that the answer to loneliness is isolation. It's really not that funny. In fact, it might seem to make sense. When you have experienced loss, betrayal, and disappointment in relationships, why risk more, even if you might actually get what you are really hungry for? Potato chips are a lot safer.

The isolation in Laurie's story is clear, even though she would say that she had a lot of friends. She couldn't connect with her husband without being under the influence. They both knew that this was false intimacy but decided it was as good as they could get. She couldn't be honest with her friends in Bible study, so although she felt convicted about her alcohol use while participating in the study, she also felt more alone, because she didn't think she could tell anyone. Her feelings of aloneness only justified her drinking. She was starting to believe that wine was her only true friend. That's how addiction gets into our bones. We can't live with it, but we can't live without it either.

Laurie eventually disclosed to me that her greatest guilt was over her mothering. She was often not available to help her children with homework or to talk to them about their lives. With shame written all over her face, she told me of the time she awakened her son for school in the morning and asked him if he had completed his book report. He replied, "Mom, I read it to you last night, but I guess you don't remember that. You don't remember anything about me."

My mind immediately went to the French children's story *The Little*

Prince. The main character in the story asks the Tippler, "Why do you drink?" The Tippler responds, "Because I feel guilty." The Little Prince immediately asks, "Why do you feel guilty?" His response highlights the vicious cycle in addiction: "Because I drink."

Addiction theorists explain the increasing power of addiction through the mechanisms of tolerance and withdrawal. Tolerance means that the user needs more and more of the same substance to get a desired affect. Withdrawal means that stopping use of the substance produces such severe consequences that the user can't imagine not using again. Tolerance and withdrawal are most often displayed in physical symptoms. The substance abuser will experience anxiety, heart palpitations, sweats, and insomnia, to name just a few of the terrible physical symptoms associated with alcohol or drug withdrawal.

I also think of tolerance and withdrawal in terms of the emotional life. Addiction seems to make my pain, stress, boredom, and loneliness more tolerable. Therefore, withdrawal from an addictive central activity intensifies the emotional distress, making the addiction seem like the only way to stay in my own skin. As consequences from the addiction increase, the pain and guilt increase as well, making a further commitment to the addiction seem like the only answer.

After stopping her drinking for two weeks, Laurie came into my office and described her emotional withdrawal. "Now I know why I drink. My marriage is lifeless. My kids are out of control, and all of my friends seem to have it so much more together than I do. I feel guiltier than ever." That night Laurie refilled her Big Gulp cup.

I Am Unforgivable

Addictions take us into the labyrinth of darkness, into stories of shame and unthinkable circumstances. For addicts and their family members, telling their stories of addiction takes tremendous courage. One of my dear clients saw me over a two-year period as we came up with strategies for her to deal with her husband's alcoholism. The true stories of this attractive, upwardly mobile couple would have been shocking to their friends and relatives— stories of drunk driving, passing out at social events, and lubricated arguments filled with hateful words. I did not see this client for about a year, and then she called to come back in for an appointment. I could feel the shame as she entered the room. I cautiously asked, "What has happened?"

She could barely get out the words, "We've had a child." Her shame at bringing a baby into this addicted family almost kept her from seeking further help. We will examine the addicted family in more detail in later chapters, but it is important to note here that it is not just the addict who struggles with a sense of being unforgivable. Often family members suffer equally, if not more. The family members' sense of shame highlights the last addiction—the addiction to ourselves—because family and friends of the addict often erroneously believe, "*I* should have done something. *I* should be able to stop this. If *I* just knew what to do, what to say, how to be, the addict would get better."

The evidence of addiction that makes us believe we are unforgivable raises a crucial question: if we can be forgiven, where does healing forgiveness come from? Certainly addicts and their family members need to be able to forgive themselves, but often that forgiveness is superficial and does not reach the heart. It comes out of wounded self-love, out of sorrow over weakness, over personal failure, or over getting caught. Such self-forgiveness often is merely an acknowledgment that we are not as good as we or others thought we were, and results in a determination to not do the same wrong again, in the hope that our better selves are strong enough to win over our addicted selves.

One of my assignments when I was in treatment was to look at myself in the mirror every day and repeat, "Sharon, I forgive you." At first, I could barely look at myself. I hated myself. Compassion and acceptance did grow during that time, but by the end of a week, I looked myself in the eyes and said, "Sharon, you don't have the power to forgive yourself." I knew that family and friends would forgive me, but there were things they didn't know about or understand. I knew I needed something More, something Other than myself.

Laurie's repeated determination to not drink came out of a fierce desire to prove herself, but that only fueled her addiction. Every time that she willed herself to be better, she would last for a while. Then she'd start feeling the realities of her life and a desire to escape from herself, and the only escape that she knew was alcohol. Repeated attempts to stop drinking only added to Laurie's guilt and left her mired in the quicksand of believing that she could never be forgiven. In his essay "A Reflection on Guilt," Dominic Maruca answers the question about the origin of healing forgiveness: "The memory of things past is indeed a worm that does not die. Whether it continues to grow by gnawing away at our hearts or is metamorphosed into a brightly colored winged creature depends…on whether we can find a forgiveness that we cannot bestow on ourselves."[7]

I AM HOPELESS

Most addicts and their families try again and again to change. They try everything. Whenever an addict attempts to change, there are consequences—a stress reaction that results in disequilibrium. What is confusing and discouraging to many addicts and their families is that once help is sought, most addictions will get worse before they get better.

In her funny and poignant account of coming face to face with her own addiction, Anne Lamott describes this process of often taking one step forward and several steps back:

One day in 1985, I woke up so hungover that I felt pinned to the bed by centrifugal force. I was in the sleeping loft of my little house-boat in Sausalito. The sun was pouring in and the birds were singing and I was literally glued to my pillow by drool. I decided to quit drinking. And I was doing quite well, remarkably well, in fact, until five o'clock that first night. Then the panic set in. Thankfully, I had a moment of clarity in which I understood that the problem was not that I drank so much but that I drank too quickly. The problem was with *pacing*. So I had a good idea. I would limit myself to two beers a night. Two beers! What a great idea!…

By the fifth day, though, after drinking the first of my [two beers], I began to resent anyone's attempts to control me—even my own. And so, as an act of liberation, I bought a fifth of Bush-mills Irish Whiskey and had drunk it all by dawn.[8]

This piece of evidence compels us to ask the questions: What is hope? What is the pleasure that moves our hearts? Paradoxically, for the addict, hope is often found in the central activity that also eventually destroys hope. The good thing (wine, sugar, sex, etc.) goes very, very bad. It ends pleasure. By contrast, my friend, psychologist and author Dr. Dan Allender, says that "by tasting a good donut, there's something that brings you to a heart that has a taste for more goodness."[9] True hope moves forward. An addict will never change unless something in his or her heart begins to hope apart from the addiction. Part of the power of hearing stories of other addicts is borrowing from their hope. When I have been stuck in the momentum of an addiction, it is hard to believe that there is hope for rest, pleasure, or relief apart from the addiction. For the addict, life becomes narrowed down to one thing, and it feels like that one thing is saving his or her life even while it destroys it. We borrow hope when we listen to the stories of other addicts who have let go of their central activity—risked drowning—only to discover new life. Sometimes the hope that pulls us out of addiction is merely holding on to another's story of redemption.

Laurie came to acknowledge that she began almost every day with no hope except that she could "unplug" with her cup of wine at the end of the day. Every time she tried to change and every avenue of change only seemed to confirm that there was no hope apart from her end-of-the-day escape.

PUTTING THE PIECES BACK TOGETHER AGAIN

Over the course of several months, Laurie had no problem identifying the evidence of addiction in her life. She felt crazy at times, alone most of the time, unforgivable when she was honest with herself, and hopeless of ever changing herself. I took a risk with Laurie and decided to confront her with one more tangible piece of evidence that addiction was at work in her life. Throughout my work with her I wondered: what would Love do with all this evidence? I remembered my own story of craziness—crouching at the trash cans by the curb, drinking straight from the bottle. Initially, that story had only brought me shame, confirming that I was alone, unforgivable, and hopeless.

> We name you by your name…. Hear our prayer for…[we] grow weary of the battering and the vicious cycles that devour us.
>
> —WALTER BRUEGGEMANN,
> *Awed to Heaven, Rooted in Earth*[10]

After many months of telling my own stories of addiction and listening to the stories of others who were courageously facing their addictions, a dear friend challenged me to imagine Someone meeting me at the curb in love. At first, I couldn't imagine *anyone* meeting me there. And then I imagined Someone, a God whose names are Hope and Love, crouching beside me and kindly handing me a beautiful crystal goblet, whispering, "Sharon, drink out of this. You weren't made for bottles hidden in brown paper bags smelling of the fish you had last night for dinner."

At Laurie's next appointment I prepared to show her a little hope, although at first she didn't see it that way. Sitting on the coffee table next to the couch in my office were four glasses of grape juice. As soon as Laurie walked in the office and saw the glasses, she suspected what I was trying to visualize.

"That is approximately how much you drink every night," I said, confirming her suspicion. "The Big Gulp holds thirty-two ounces; that's more than four glasses of wine, which are four to six ounces each," I explained. "According to the *Diagnostic and Statistical Manual,* four glasses of wine a night classify you as abusing alcohol."

"I already know that," Laurie mumbled.

Then I offered her a crystal goblet rimmed with gold at the top. "Let me give you this. If you're going to drink," I said, "why don't you drink out of this? You were made for more than Big Gulp plastic."

Was I encouraging Laurie, probably an alcoholic, to drink? Not at all. But I wanted to catch her in more than her guilt and shame. I wanted to catch her in acceptance, grace, and love. I hoped to give her a human taste of the Love that heals with a picture of hope, that she was made for More than she was experiencing. For Laurie, this actually began the redemptive process. She acknowledged her addiction to her friends and family. With their support, she began attending Twelve Step meetings. She hasn't drunk for over four years. She would tell you that for her, redemption began with the gift of being caught.

2

THE GIFT OF GETTING CAUGHT

The hardness of God is greater than the kindness of man,
for His compulsion is our liberation.
—C. S. LEWIS, *Surprised by Joy*

I f there is one theme in my own story that surfaces again and again, it is the theme of getting caught. Caught. Perhaps this idea stirs memories for you as it does for me—my mother catching me in a lie, a teacher catching me unprepared, or a friend overhearing my careless words.

In the spring of 2001 I was attending a fund-raiser for a crisis pregnancy center in our area. As I was milling about the crowd before the program began, I overheard someone talking about *me*. I decided to remain undisclosed and listen to what I hoped would be my accolades. It was actually one of my newer clients describing her impressions of me. She continued, "My counselor is really helping me with my eating disorder, because she actually had an eating disorder." I braced myself for further praise about how helpful I had been. "My counselor is a recovering alcoholic and really understands addiction. My counselor is going through a painful divorce…" She paused for a moment and then concluded, "I think my counselor has had everything described in the *DSM-IV [Diagnostic and Statistical Manual of Mental Disorders]!*"

I was caught.

Does your heart beat faster and your foot press heavily on the brakes when you see a state patrolman? Then you are like 88 percent of the population.[1] It seems we are all quick to slow down when we fear getting caught.

Do you ever dream that you arrive at school or work and are not appropriately clothed, and you rush around to find the right clothes before someone notices? Then you are like 65 percent of the population.[2] Some dream analysts suggest that this dream reveals that we don't believe that we are authentic and we fear being found out.

Do you live with the sense that if anyone really knew you, that person could not bear to be in relationship with you? Then you are like 97 percent of those questioned in one Leadership Institute Survey.[3] We are all afraid of being caught and even more afraid of its consequences.

If these statistics are right—whether you are an addict or family member—in life's game of tag, every one of you reading this book believes that you are "it," but most of us are afraid to admit it.

There is a story in the New Testament that describes most poignantly the experience of a person who is caught. Let me paraphrase it for you.

Two men led her into a room filled with people she didn't know. When they first entered the room, she thought they might let her sit quietly at the back, since the meeting had already begun. But the two men marched her to the front, and all eyes shifted from the speaker to her. Her face flushed during this conspicuous entrance, and she fought to hold back tears of fear and humiliation. She could not believe this was happening.

The night before, she'd slipped out of her own house to meet a man for a midnight tryst. She knew it was wrong and even dangerous, but the thrill of his touch and the comfort of his kindness enticed her to dismiss her nagging conscience and ignore the possible consequences. Her heart beat faster as she remembered their passionate embrace…and then the loud knock at the door. It had all happened so quickly. Men she recognized as important leaders in their community rushed into the room. They commanded her to gather her belongings and to come with them immediately. They'd escorted her through the city, arriving at the meeting at dawn.

She glanced at the man seated at the front of the room and wondered if he was to be her judge. She looked into his eyes imploringly as her escorts told her to stand and face the group. Slowly she turned and saw the crowd sitting on the edge of their seats, staring at her. One of her accusers addressed the man sitting before them: "Teacher, this woman was caught red-handed in the act of adultery. Moses, in the Law, gives orders to stone such persons. What do you say?"[4]

We feel for her. Caught by the police, by our parents, by our spouse, by health, legal, or financial consequences, or by our employer—to be caught is a gift that seems unwelcome at first. In the last chapter I told you about Laurie and her experience of being caught in my office looking at four goblets of grape juice, a representation of her nightly Big Gulp cup of wine.

When you feel the sting of humiliation that often comes with being caught, it's hard to believe that it is a gift. But even the humiliation is a gift. It will either send us scrambling back to our oblivion to forget our failure and shame, or it will humble us enough to receive what is possible only when we are caught: *to be known, to be forgiven, and to still be wanted.*

THE ADDICT IS CAUGHT

In order to fully connect this New Testament story with our own, we need to see that there are four people caught in this story. Four people who have the opportunity to receive the gift of being caught—a gift that comes all too often in the midst of addiction. We won't have any trouble identifying the first character that is caught in the story: the adulteress. It is possible that she was a sex addict. According to author Marnie C. Ferree, one of every six women struggles with sexual addiction: "Women, far more than men, are likely to act out their behaviors [sexual addictions] in real life, such as having multiple partners, casual sex, or affairs."[5] Whether we are addicts or not, we can easily identify this woman as caught. That's the reality of addiction; its truth always comes out.

Congressmen, celebrities, and religious leaders all get caught in the consequences of addiction. The headlines shouldn't surprise us. Having the "good life" doesn't keep us from disappointing relationships, personal failures, unfulfilled longings, or impulsive mistakes. However, we seldom leap directly into an addiction. Most often we begin by experimenting with behaviors that initially promise to be satisfying, soothing, or within our control. We gradually relinquish not only our longings but our wills to these behaviors. We become willing to sacrifice time, judgment, healthy relationships, even our spiritual lives to the overtly destructive or subtly deadening addictions. We may end up like the woman in the story, caught by choices and behaviors that have taken control of our lives.

But most of us are better at hiding than that.

Which brings us to the second person caught in the story.

THE NOT-SO-EASILY-IDENTIFIED ADDICT IS CAUGHT

To use the New Testament term, this is the collective Pharisee. The woman's accusers have taken her in the act and dragged her to judgment. Her accuser is the person clothed in accomplishments, reputation, eloquence, even piety—clothed in the security of being respectable. In the story that unfolds after the woman is brought before the room full of men, Jesus looks at her accusers and says, "If any one of you is without sin, let him be the first to throw a stone at her" (John 8:7, NIV).

And the Pharisee is caught. In the lightning-bolt look from Jesus, he knows that beneath his clothes and reputation and pretension and religion, he is naked too—stripped as bare as the woman he has exposed. The text records, "At this, those who heard began to go away one at a time, the older ones first, until only Jesus was left, with the woman still standing there" (verse 9).

Here is the tragedy in the story.

One by one they slipped away—all of them knowing that they had secrets too, but slinking away in silence, not disclosing their struggles to one another, because they could not admit that they were like the caught woman.

I believe that John told this story of the struggling, stumbling woman to reveal the story of the hiding, self-righteous Pharisee. The gift of some addictions is that often we get caught. They give us away: our weaving driving, our slurring speech, our dwindling bank accounts, and our health problems.

For the man or woman addicted to pleasing people, working too much, or doing everything perfectly, however, this gift is often much longer in arriving. Although the consequences might not seem so severe, these addictions also narrow life down until there is really no living—existence maybe, but no living. In one psychological study on addiction to perfection, the author explains, "All day the mask, or persona, performs with perfect efficiency, but when the job is done, those frenzied, foreign rhythms continue to dominate body and Being." The author continues to describe these addictions as gods that "demand perfection—perfect efficiency, perfect world, perfect clean, perfect body, perfect bones, but they being human, and not prime-time TV advertisements, falter into perfect chaos and perfect death. [This god] obliterates them and, being obliterated, they at last fall asleep."[6]

Caught. The verdict is the same for the woman in her adultery and for the respectable men slinking away in silence. I think this story is our story. It is not meant to be merely instructional or inspirational, but primarily incarnational. The Great Teacher used the unclothed adulteress as a gracious and kind visual aid. She eloquently and agonizingly illustrates that no matter how hard we try to be good or how well we hide our failures, we are all helpless.

I found myself caught in the middle between these two realities in my own life. Even though I was a Christian woman who cared deeply about God and my family, I fell in love with alcohol. In my early twenties I began experiencing what I now know were panic attacks. The tensions of marriage, the loneliness of living two thousand miles away from family and friends, and my intense desire to keep it all together and look good combined to produce a roller coaster of emotions that I was not equipped to handle and a thirst that I was desperate to quench.

A well-meaning doctor prescribed a glass of wine to soothe my mounting internal tension. Alcohol had never been a part of my life, but I was desperate for some relief from the pain, loneliness, and inner stress. I experienced the benefits of alcohol immediately, the temporary satiation of my emotional thirst.

> My soul thirsts for you,
> my body longs for you,
> in a dry and weary land
> where there is no water.
>
> —A PSALM OF DAVID[7]

It erased tension, eased my loneliness, and relaxed my uptight tendencies. The habitual glass of wine turned into a daily dose of harder liquor that turned into a compulsion that stealthily crept into my daily life. I found that alcohol made everything better, until it made everything worse.

What an incongruous collage of images filled my life at that time. In my garage were Christmas tins packed for the elderly by women's meetings at my church and trash cans crammed with empty vodka bottles. Sunday school lessons faithfully prepared and articulately delivered, and at home, lubricated arguments laced with awful words that could never be taken back. Regular

attendance at all church functions, and years of anesthetized pain and pleasure. Mine was a life immersed in the church and splashed with booze.

I knew that my relationships with family, friends, and God were dete-
riorating, but I vigorously denied my problem. I felt awful about myself
but refused to look openly and honestly at my life. I was afraid that if people knew the truth about me, they would be shocked and disgusted.

I understand the tension in the story between the woman and the
Pharisees. We are afraid that if people really knew us, they couldn't handle
the truth, and so we hide.

Slowly, I began to get caught. I couldn't function in my daily life because sometimes I was too hung over. Friends started to report strange telephone calls from me, where I talked on and on. My young children began
to ask incessantly, "Mommy, are you sick?" One day, my parents found me
completely out of it, under the influence, and took me to a detox facility
where I stayed for three days. And then I sought help. I was so deeply
humiliated by being caught, trapped in a lockdown facility where I couldn't
even hold my own Chapstick, surrounded by alcoholics and addicts who
had serious problems, that I drove clear across town to a private counselor,
confessed my habit, and stopped drinking.

Yes, I just stopped. There was about a week of misery, but I stopped.
Whew! I could go back into hiding. No one needed to know, and if I ever
decided to tell the story, it would be *years* down the road. I would be a different person by then.

Although I'd been caught, I didn't receive the gift. I didn't ask myself
what would happen if life fell through the cracks or my dreams shattered.

And then in 2001 my life did fall through the cracks. My marriage fell
apart. I was ashamed and afraid, and I foolishly thought that alcohol could
put the pieces back together again. I relapsed. I didn't know the sobering
statistics reported by addiction expert Robert Perkinson, that 95 percent of
untreated addicts die in their addiction.[8] That weekend, I was supposed to

teach a Sunday school class at my church. I called Aram, the pastor for congregational care, to confirm the details for the Sunday class. He called me back a few minutes later and with love in his voice said, "Sharon, it sounds to me like you have been drinking."

I was caught.

Aram may have saved my life. But he certainly reintroduced to me this gift of being caught, of being known, forgiven, and still wanted. I confessed my relapse and sought help. I began attending Alcoholics Anonymous meetings. And a few weeks later, I received a referral of a new client to my counseling office—from Aram. Known. Forgiven. Still wanted.

I wish that I could tell you that I will never again forget my vulnerability to worshiping a god that will ultimately destroy me. I've stumbled a lot along the way. But I do get caught. Even if it's not alcohol, I get caught. Caught in my capacity to deceive and my willingness to be deceived. Caught in my loving of things and my using of people. Caught in my longing for position and the shrinking of my soul. Caught in my clamor for privilege and my silence at injustice.

It's easy to walk away from looking at the truth when there aren't a lot of consequences. Unlike the shamed woman caught in adultery, disobedience, and immorality, the Pharisee is caught in his piety, obedience, and morality, making it not only easy but seemingly reasonable for him to walk away, until just Jesus and the woman were standing there.

Which brings us to the third person caught in the story.

LOVE IS CAUGHT

The text tells us that Jesus was initially seated, teaching, when the men brought the adulteress to the front of the crowd. "Teacher," they said, "this woman was caught in the act of adultery. In the Law Moses commanded us to stone such women. Now what do you say?" (John 8:4–5, NIV).

He was caught. They had Him, didn't they? Caught with the very words of Scripture.

After their accusation Jesus bent down to write something in the dirt. The crowd continued to hammer Him with questions and accusations about her crime and punishment. Jesus stood up, looked at them, and said, "If any one of you is without sin, let him be the first to throw a stone at her" (verse 7). Again, Jesus stooped down before the woman and wrote on the ground.

Now I have heard pastors and theologians debate and preach entire sermons on what Jesus wrote in the dirt, but I cannot get past His gesture of kneeling before the woman while everyone was expecting an execution.

And then at last, after everyone filed out, Jesus straightened Himself and asked, "Woman, where are they? Has no one condemned you?"

"No one, sir," she said.

"Then neither do I condemn you. Go now and leave your life of sin" (verses 10–11).

I understand from those who have studied the historical context of this story that this was an invitation of great honor. "Go" is the same invitation in Jesus's commission to His inner circle, His disciples: "Go into all the world."[9] To this woman the word is an invitation, "Go—join the others. You are wanted."

Can you imagine all that stirred in this woman's heart? She looked into the eyes of the man she thought was to be her judge, and received a gift. Don't you just wish one of those Pharisees had hung around and seen for himself the unforeseeable? The gift of being caught is at the worst possible time, what needs to happen, what we believe can't possibly happen, does impossibly happen. What happens is grace—to be known, to be forgiven, and to still be wanted.

This story gives me joy and hope as I think about my own experience with addiction and the many addicts I have worked with. Too many times the terrible behavior of the addict pushes away family and friends. They don't want to get caught in the mess of the addict. Who can blame them? That's why this story is so amazing. It embodies the Love that has been looking for us all our lives, the Love we have been looking for as well. In this story, *Jesus is longing to be caught too.* To be Known. To be Loved. To still be wanted. As He looked with forgiveness into the eyes of the woman, I believe He also looked with longing: *Do you want me?*

In December 2005 I traveled to Cambodia with my nineteen-year-old daughter, Kristin. On Christmas Day, we were in the village of Anlong Veng. For almost a decade this was the ultimate of Khmer Rouge strongholds, home of Pol Pot, the most notorious leader of Democratic Kampuchea. It is located in the most primitive jungle part of Cambodia. Most of the people in this community had never left their villages. They were afraid—afraid of discrimination, retaliation, and hatred, because their ancestors were the ones who had orchestrated the killing fields of Cambodia. Their parents and grandparents were the Nazis of Southeast Asia.

For Christmas, we attended an open-air church service with about three hundred Cambodians and their children and animals. The congregation sang with gusto (and no accompaniment) the songs of Christmas. The children lined up behind the platform and waited excitedly to perform the Nativity story,

> I am the vessel.
> The draught is God's.
> And God is the thirsty one.
>
> —DAG HAMMARSKJOLD[10]

giggling and pointing at their parents. As they solemnly recited their lines and played their parts, I felt like I was seeing the Christmas story for the first time. I have never experienced such joy in all my life. When the performance ended, all three hundred of us, sitting amid dogs, goats, and one pig, jumped to our feet to give a standing ovation.

Later I asked our guide about the powerful emotions of this meeting. She explained, "Oh, they believe God is the only One who wants them, and so they want Him."

It is not always the holy and devout or the emotionally well balanced who come to understand Love. In order to receive the gift of getting caught, we must be able to acknowledge, with the powerlessness and poverty of a little child, that we can't free ourselves. We must be set free by the love of the One whose names are liberty, mercy, freedom, release, grace, hope, and peace.

FINALLY CAUGHT

Which brings us to the fourth person caught in this story. Do you see him? or her? Because it is you and me, the reader.

Someone once asked the great contemplative Thomas Merton, "Who are you?" He answered immediately, "I am the loved one."[11]

What keeps you from immediately answering as Merton did? The bondage of addiction? Humiliating circumstances? Family members who seem to love their addictions more than they love you? Or maybe it's your accomplishments, responsibilities, and performance.

When my son Graham was four years old, he was fascinated with knives (he's now nineteen and still fascinated!). He loved to look at and hold a sharp knife that we used to clean fish. In order to keep Graham out of harm's way, we put the knife in a cupboard above the refrigerator. One day I walked into the kitchen and saw that Graham had pushed a chair over by the counter. He had climbed up on the chair, onto the counter, and on top of the refrigerator to reach the cupboard. When I walked into the kitchen, he was standing on the countertop holding the knife.

"Graham!" I exclaimed. "You know you're not supposed to have that."

And then I said what mothers everywhere say: "Graham, even if I had never found out about this—*God would have known.*"

I think often of Graham's reply. "Why?" he wondered. "Why is God always watching *me?*"

Why is God always watching us?

We learn as children that God knows when we lie or fight with our siblings. God knows when we don't listen in church. When we reach adolescence, we learn that God is especially watching if we even think about sex, drinking, or drugs. I recall one of my students finally talking about his hidden addiction. He explained it this way: "I have put all of this in a secret box in my heart that I haven't shown anyone—even God." Then he looked at the floor in shame and said, "I guess God already knew."

Why is God always watching us? I'm afraid the impression we've been given by many well-meaning religious institutions is that God is watching so that He can humiliate us, punish us, and whip us back into shape. According to the Leadership Institute survey that I mentioned at the beginning of this chapter, 97 percent of those surveyed believe that it is too good to be true that there is Someone who really knows us, forgives us, and still wants to be in relationship with us.

The gift of getting caught is that we might come face to face with Love—a Love greater than human love—that knows us, knows our horrible struggles, knows our hidden struggles, and loves us and longs to forgive us. God loves us. *That's why He's always watching.*

For just a moment now, allow yourself to sit here and be caught—in all your secrets and goodness, your failings and achievements. Can you allow Love to look deeply into your soul, see Love stoop before you, and read what Love is writing?

I believe there is one word.

Beloved.

Not addict. Not alcoholic, hopeless relapser, gambler, or compulsive overeater.

Beloved.

The gift of getting caught—when we don't do it all right and can't prove our worth—is realizing that being beloved is the core of our existence. We are loved when we are good for nothing! The purest parallel to this is when we first come into the world, really good for nothing. All a baby does is eat, sleep, and dirty diapers. But most babies are born into being loved while they are good for nothing. Beloved. This is our identity. It is the word written to the woman caught in her publicly exposed addiction. It is the word written to the man caught in his hidden addiction.

What keeps us from receiving this gift? When I was first caught in my alcoholism, I missed the gift because I did not stay to hear Love speak. I was too busy with the last addiction, trying to prove myself with myself by myself.

The Giver longs for us to receive this gift. As Richard Foster wrote, "Today the heart of God is an open wound of love. He aches over our distance and preoccupation. He mourns that we do not draw near to him. He grieves that we have forgotten him. He weeps over our obsession with muchness and manyness. He longs for our presence."[12]

The surprising and oh-so-relieving gift of getting caught is that Love simply longs for our presence, when we are too weak and wounded to do anything to make ourselves lovable.

God pursues us. Sometimes silently and sometimes shouting. The light of His love is sometimes dimmed and sometimes glaring. He uses our struggles and our self-sufficiency to catch us and reveal our need of Love.

Is getting caught The Answer to addiction? Obviously not. For there are many who have been caught, arrested, and hospitalized who return to their addictions. But being caught by Love opens the heart to the hint that there might be More. And that is the beginning.

3

The Energy and Experience of Addiction

It is the nature of desire not to be satisfied, and most
[human beings] live only for the gratification of it.
—Aristotle

Brian doesn't look like an addict. He wears starched shirts and polished shoes. He drives a 2006 Lexus LX470. But Brian can't sleep at night. He often arises before 4:30 a.m. and leaves his home while his wife and children are fast asleep. He's begun experiencing chest pains, and he finds that the only way he can relax and interact with his family is after two glasses of wine. He is irritable and short with everyone, feels like most people in his life take him for granted, and finds himself withdrawing from any close friends.

What is it? Drug addiction? Maybe cocaine? An extramarital affair? No, Brian is addicted to work. He works over fifty-five hours every week, and when he's not at work, he's thinking about work. He has built his own company from the ground up and is proud of his accomplishments, but he feels the pull of the "golden handcuffs" every day. He can't stop. He is in too deep.

Workaholism is one of those behaviors that is hard to classify as a serious addiction. After all, according to the Bureau of Labor Statistics, the average American works 49 hours per week; that turns out to be 350 more hours per year than the average European. Expedia.com reports that 12 percent of Americans never take a vacation.[1]

We really don't want workaholics sitting around on folding chairs in church basements confessing their addiction and trying to stop working so much. That might limit productivity. Unless, of course, that workaholic is you or a family member. Workaholism has the same costs as any other addiction; relational, physical, and spiritual consequences are part of the toll we pay for being so productive. According to Diane Fassel, author of *Working Ourselves to Death,* "workaholism affects all walks of life, not just high-powered executives, and it can affect physical health. Often a workaholic will die before an alcoholic."[2]

When Brian and his wife first came to see me, they described the treadmill they were on and the toll it was taking on their family. Brian finally said in exasperation, "I don't have any choice. Sure, everyone says that they want me home more, but they would be sorry if I stopped bringing in the money."

His wife snapped, "You couldn't stay home if you tried. Work is your escape from everything else."

This couple clearly exposed the cunning nature of addiction. If addiction is primarily obsession and compulsion, then whenever you feel like you don't have a choice, you are in the radar of an addiction, even if that choice might look like a good thing. Remember that every addiction is a good thing gone bad—desire gone awry. Brian's story also highlights the powerful energy that is a part of every addiction. Addiction becomes the central activity—the momentum of life—because something gives it energy. At the heart of every addiction are two jolts of charge: the belief that I deserve escape and the fact that I demand control.

THE GREAT ESCAPE

It might not look like Brian is escaping at all. In fact, he says that he feels trapped. Understanding the three components of the great escape reveals how Brian fuels his workaholism with an energy that might look good on the outside, but on the inside he risks losing his own soul. Workaholism forfeits the wisdom that comes from struggling within messy relationships, the strength that is

> What good would it do to get everything you want and lose you, the real you? What could you ever trade your soul for?
>
> —THE GOSPEL OF MARK[3]

forged by dealing with our human weaknesses, and the healing that comes when we risk giving and receiving love.

I Want Relief from the Struggles of Living in a Messy World

The Greeks believed that the gods gave them wine so that they might forget the misery of their existence. This is what maintains an addiction—it initially provides relief, and the addict continues to try to re-create that initial experience. Life is sorrowful; we taste it daily in grief, fear, loneliness, shame, and longing. Addiction provides a means of fleeing the depths of reality for a more palatable world. When Brian spends fifty-five-plus hours a week consumed by his work, he doesn't need to think about his wife's loneliness, his daughter's heartbreak with her boyfriend, or his friends' failure to support him.

Brian's escape may actually look more like turmoil than relief. That's what addiction does; it exchanges one passion for another, lesser passion. When Brian spends all of his passion at the office, he doesn't have much passion left for messy relationships. Even in workaholism there is immediate gratification. The minute I turn on my computer and begin writing, I leave behind the dirty laundry, my daughter's angst over her major in college, and my worries about my aging parents.

When I first began speaking about addiction, I did a radio call-in program in the Denver area. One woman called in and asked with frustration, "Don't we deserve a break sometimes?" Of course we do. But only an addict would consider fifty-five hours of work a week, a hangover every morning, or the loss of relationships due to a destructive central activity as a break. I often think of this when I travel to Orlando, Florida, where I go twice a year to teach. When my children were younger, I would take them to the theme parks Orlando is famous for. As we stood in lines for hours sweating profusely, spent over three hundred dollars a day on recreation, and listened to countless children crying from exhaustion and parents yelling from exasperation, I thought, *Only in our culture do we consider this a vacation!*

I Want a Temporary Exit from the Human Condition

This energy of the great escape really began in the first story God tells about humans. When Adam and Eve were tempted with forbidden fruit, the idea that energized their behavior was "You will be like God."[4] They wanted to be more than they were, more than they had been made to be. We replicate their choice when we use a mood-altering substance or experience to provide relief from shyness, from the tension or awkwardness in a relationship, or from the fear of incompetence in any arena. Addiction offers us an escape from being human.

In his masterful fiction on alcoholism, Jack London describes the exit from humanness that alcohol can temporarily give a person:

My brain was illuminated by the clear, white light.… I was a lord
of thought, the master of my vocabulary and of the totality of my
experience.… For so [i]t tricks and lures, setting the maggots

of intelligence gnawing, whispering his fatal intuitions of truth,
flinging purple passages into the monotony of one's days.[5]

The path into the labyrinth of addiction is well traveled and sometimes
looks respectable, but like alcoholism, workaholism is a deadly and deadening addiction. Brian justified his escape through workaholism like this:
"Nobody gets it. Everyone just goes about their lives without a thought for
how hard I work. That's why I have pulled away from everyone." Brian's
false sense of superiority kept him from feeling everything else and kept
him isolated.

The New Testament tells a story of two men that illustrates both the
energy of addiction and its antidote in the context of another respectable
addiction—religion:

The Energy of Addiction:

Two men went up to the Temple to pray, one a Pharisee, the other
a tax man. The Pharisee posed and prayed like this: "Oh, God, I
thank you that I am not like other people—robbers, crooks, adulter-
ers, or, heaven forbid, like this tax man. I fast twice a week and tithe
on all my income."

An Antidote to Addiction:

Meanwhile the tax man, slumped in the shadows, his face in his
hands, not daring to look up, said, "God, give mercy."[6]

The irony is that sooner or later, our addictions will prove to us that we
are not gods, and they may allow us to turn to God with a true sense of who
we are, with an integrity that is both humble and confident. We will talk
about this gift of surrender in the next chapter.

I Want to Be Let Off the Hook from the Cost of Loving

The deepest relief that addiction provides is that it destroys our deepest passions. As addiction continues, it dulls the deeper passions of our hearts for other people and other things. Addiction opposes love. It nails the energy of our longings to someone or something—a person, place, substance, behavior, or belief. And the addictive object or central activity works; it provides relief from living in the midst of messy relationships, so we want more and more of it. But then it imprisons us in self-hatred.

Brian told me what happened one night when he was tucking his youngest son into bed. His son said, "Daddy, why aren't you ever here?" Brian felt the familiar irritation at everyone's lack of gratitude for what he did.

"Because I have to work," he answered sharply.

"No, I mean when you're here, you're not even here. Daddy, you don't know me, and I don't know you." His son had been able to see the cost of his father's addiction.

Brian looked at me and for the first time began to pierce the denial about his addiction: "I want to live differently. I hate how I'm living and what I'm doing to my children, but I am afraid."

When we are addicted, we cannot love. We must be able to pay attention in order to love others, and attention is kidnapped by addiction.

The great escape can be summed up in this vicious cycle: "I believe that I deserve an escape, so I will choose the fastest, most predictable, most accessible, and most effective route available, and I will end up with more pain and problems, hating myself more, and feeling shame, thus further limiting my capacity to love…so, I deserve an escape."

I Demand Control

Every addiction is a way of saying to God, "I don't like what You've created. I'll take over." Addiction is the ultimate effort to control—control pain and self-consciousness, forget mistakes, and even find easy spirituality. When my children were young, we attended a church that invited all the children to the front of the auditorium at the beginning of the service for the children's sermon. One Sunday the pastor asked the children, "If you were God, what would you do?" Quickly, my five-year-old son, already aware that he was larger than most kids his age, answered, "If I were God, I'd make all the food with no fat in it, so that you could eat whatever you want!"

Like my son, we often imagine that we know better than God. Addiction is energized by the belief that if God were as He should be, we would not struggle with desire and having to say no to desire. And so we substitute a god of our own making. Really, the heart of addiction is rooted in the last addiction: "I will be in charge, because I know best."

We will look at eating addictions in depth later on, but every eating addiction is a model for all addictions, a defiant response to the Old Testament words: "[God] humbled you, causing you to hunger and then feeding you with manna…to teach you that man does not live on bread alone but on every word that comes from the mouth of the LORD."[8] Consider the energy of a person struggling with bulimia, a binge-and-purge eat-

> Woe to the man so possessed that he thinks he possesses God!
>
> —MARTIN BUBER[7]

ing addiction: "I will not be humbled. I will not feel hunger. I will not trust your food or your feeding schedule. I will live on bread alone, but since you are so stupid as to put fat in it, I will take care of that also."

We can tell where Brian was in control—in control of his business, his finances, his employees, his schedule—and where he was out of control—out of control of his feelings, his relationships, his time, and his anger. In control. Out of control. Remember, when you are in relationship with an addict who shows symptoms of an out-of-control life, his or her initial desire was to be in control.

In her beautifully written book *Holy Hunger*, Margaret Bullitt-Jonas describes the powerful energy of addiction—escape and control:

> So I eat. I eat. I eat past the point of being physically full. I eat until I'm stuffed. I eat until I hurt. I eat until I feel nothing, until I'm numb, until I'm weary of eating and can eat nothing more.
>
> A triumphant, angry mind, gripped by addiction, and a sorrowing, suffering body.[9]

THE EXPERIENCE OF ADDICTION: KILLING TIME

When we are energized by the desires for escape and control, the experience of addiction dominates our sense of time. Living in the fullness of time includes the ability to redemptively remember your past (faith), to dream about the future (hope), and to remain rooted in the present (love). Addiction keeps us from living in the fullness of time, because life is gradually absorbed by one thing. Faith, hope, and love are extinguished by addiction.

Like most addicted families, Brian's family didn't spend a lot of time sitting around the fireplace remembering what had built their family; they didn't have a lot of dreams for the future for individual family members. Like it or not, they all worshiped at the altar of Brian's work and sacrificed living in the fullness of time.

I said to Brian during one session, "Could it be that you were made for more than work?"

Brian shook his head, "I used to think I was, but I have forgotten anything else that I wanted."

The Past Can Be Forgotten

The addict murders time by three false beliefs. First, addictions become a partner with oblivion. There is no better example than the alcoholic who blacks out and literally cannot remember what happened that evening. Brian's oblivion is powerful in a different way—not life forgotten, but life never lived. Memory is the proof of life, and when our lives are absorbed by one thing, we can forget the pain of the past, its loss, failure, and limitations. However, then we also forget what brought us joy, anticipation, and fulfillment.

I recently attended a weekly meeting of a drug and alcohol education class at a local treatment program. During the class, we were asked to fill out a worksheet titled "All About Me." On it were three columns: Relationships, Work, and Hobbies. Out of a class of over twenty people, only two people could list any hobbies, evidence that addiction narrows life and destroys passion.

When I am in the grip of an addiction, I cannot answer the question "Who am I?" I might be able to list what I do, how I fail, or how others see me, but I cannot answer from the depths of my heart who I truly am. I have forgotten.

The Future Can Be Postponed

Second, addiction also absorbs our passion for what lies ahead. An intense focus on the object or craving narrows my perspective. If I cannot redemptively remember the past, how dare I hope for the future? Addiction tangles up the past and future in subtle and seductive ways. We were meant to

Free Beer Tomorrow

—SIGN IN SUNSET RIDGE LIQUOR STORE, WESTMINSTER, COLORADO

ask the questions "Who am I? Who will I be?" The addict, though, says, "I'll think about it tomorrow."

I asked Brian to talk about his dreams for the future. He talked for at least ten minutes about his goals for his company and financial security, and he had some vague dream of retiring and playing golf all day. Once again I asked him, "What if you were meant to be more than a successful businessman?" Brian's face was blank at first and then contorted with emotion. "I'd like to believe that, but I don't know what else I could be."

> Where there is no vision, the people perish.
>
> —A PROVERB OF SOLOMON[10]

The Present Is All That Matters

Third, the addict often believes that he or she is really living, caught in the lie that having it all now is the goal. And yet in demanding to have it all now, the addict has no now. Philosopher Søren Kierkegaard wrote about the way recreational obsessions distort time: "Time becomes a series of now-moments which must be filled with pleasurable distractions."[11]

This distortion of time takes place in the addicted family as well. Such family life emphasizes short-term stability rather than long-term growth. Family members feel trapped, and survival becomes the focus (not that different from Brian's experience of his own addiction). Spiritual growth, parenting, and dreams for the future cannot be the focus.

When the present is all that matters, you cannot answer the question "What have I become?" Friends and family of addicts often cannot understand why addicts can't see the destructive patterns that they are in. The experience of addiction—the distortion of time—fuels denial. In his book on addiction, *The Opposite of Everything Is True,* priest and recovering alcoholic William Crisman defined denial: "It is dynamic, constantly drawing energy to itself to buttress itself and expand its hold. And in a very short time, it becomes the lens through which all the awareness, feelings, and behaviors of its subjects are filtered."[12]

When denial is the lens through which we see our lives, we can't answer the questions that orient us to reality: What is it that keeps me in self-destructive behavior? Why am I experiencing loss and depression instead of fulfillment and life? Why do I seem to be drawn to the exact opposite of what I really need and want? What convinces me that I need this central activity to live? Why have I given my heart and soul to something that does not give back?

When Brian began to answer these questions honestly, he was able to see what he had become. He was an addict, no more and no less than those who gather in church basements and begin to speak by saying, "My name is…, and I'm an alcoholic."

> We crave release, but refuse to release—and so long as we cling, we are bound.
>
> —ERNEST KURTZ AND KATHERINE KETCHAM,
> *The Spirituality of Imperfection*[13]

Something mysterious happened the day when Brian began to acknowledge his idol: he received the slow and life-changing gift of surrender. As Brian acknowledged that he was addicted to work, he gave in to those truths that initially scare us to death but eventually set us free. Brian attended a two-week spiritual retreat on soul-care and learned important strategies for slowing down, stopping, and taking time away from his central activity. As he began to incorporate these strategies into his schedule, he also started paying attention to his family, noticing what they needed and wanted from him, and realizing what they had to give him.

Perhaps the most important lesson Brian learned was that he could not make these changes on his own. He found a businessmen's breakfast that incorporated spiritual study with specific application to business practices. He confessed his workaholism and discovered that he was not alone; he found many other people who felt used and used up. I asked Brian how he would describe his process of surrender. He said, "I simply let go, and that let in God and other people."

We are going to look in depth at the gift of surrender in the next chapter, but I think Brian defined the mystery of change very well. And over one hundred years ago, before the Internet, cell phones, and mergers, theologian William James also identified this process of surrendering the energy and experience of addiction: "[Surrender is] a form of regeneration by relaxing, by letting go.... It is but giving your private convulsive self a rest, and finding that a greater Self is there."[14] Surrender is the path to redeeming time.

4

THE GIFT OF SURRENDER

> In accepting ourselves, we become ourselves. As released,
> we gratefully enter into the play of which we are already
> a part. Releasement means "homecoming."
> —MICHAEL ZIMMERMAN, *Eclipse of the Self*[1]

When we stepped off the small plane in Phnom Penh, we had been traveling for two full days. We'd flown from Denver to Los Angeles to Hong Kong to Bangkok to Phnom Penh, Cambodia. My daughter Kristin and I waited by the side of the plane to gather our luggage. As we walked to the curb we saw a tiny Asian woman, Rhonda Lee, our guide. She immediately began motioning and talking fast and furiously in words we did not understand to a man beside her, a man we would later come to know and love, Tan, our translator. I assumed that they were just very happy to see us.

And then Tan got into the dusty Honda by the curb and drove off! Rhonda looked at us with big brown eyes of wonder and said, "You have so many bags. Tan go get truck."

This was the first of many lessons that we would learn from the people of Cambodia, who offered us far more than we gave to them. Tan came back with a beat-up old Ford pickup, and Kristin and I rode in the back to hold on to all our bags. As we rode through the dusty, jam-packed, busy, smelly streets of Phnom Penh, our bags were at the forefront of my mind. We were holding on to them for dear life to keep them in the truck, but also to keep us in the truck.

And I thought about surrender. This may seem like an unlikely context—right when I was fiercely holding on to things—but my mind immediately went to another unlikely setting, where I first learned about holding on and letting go, about surrender. It was a dusty, jam-packed, smelly room at the Arapahoe House, a treatment facility for drug addicts and alcoholics. The meeting room in the suburban office building had signs on the wall: "One Day at a Time," "Let Go and Let God," and "Fake It 'Til You Make It." I was taking a weekly class there as a result of the relapse I mentioned earlier, and I was fiercely holding on to my belief that *this* was the last place I needed or wanted to be.

The room was filled with people, including many who barely spoke English. A woman named Maria had tattoos across her body, big brilliant ones. I could not stop staring, and I finally asked her about the design that seemed to cover her entire chest. She explained, "It says 'Phillip.' That's the name of my ex-husband. He's in prison."

One young man always seemed to sit next to me. He had recently been released from jail and wore an ankle bracelet (not the decorative type). Every week there were new people in the class, and we all had to repeat why we were there. Every week the group leader asked this young man why he had been in jail. Every week he replied, "I'd rather not say." I'll admit that this kind of freaked me out.

I was taking this class just to make family and friends happy. I really didn't think there was a thing that they could teach me. They didn't know who I was. After all, I had written about addiction. I taught graduate classes.

THE BAGGAGE CART

During one session, we were watching a video about emotional baggage. I was bored; I had taken a whole class on that in graduate school. Now we had a worksheet called "The Baggage Cart," which we were supposed to fill out as we watched the video.

I was making a list of tasks I needed to get done the next day.

And then the woman on the video said something that woke me up. She said, "Your bags are not the main thing. Everyone has baggage. And we tend to accumulate more the older we get. What determines the quality of your life is *what you use* to carry your bags."

She had my attention. I looked around the dusty, jam-packed, smelly room, and all of a sudden, I knew that this was exactly where I needed to be. I had come to class believing that the quality of my life was determined by other people and circumstances. Her statement reminded me that my quality of life had been compromised—once again—by using alcohol to help me "carry" my difficulties and disappointments. I wasn't sure why the girl with the tattoo or the young man with the ankle bracelet was in the class, but I suspected they weren't handling the baggage of their lives very well either. We were linked by our suffering and our common mishandling of our suffering. I glanced at them and saw that *they* were paying attention. They knew that *they* needed help. And then I learned something from them. I saw something more true than a tattoo or an ankle bracelet. I saw their hearts, earnestly seeking help. Surrender began for me in a room full of beautiful wrecks.

The First Gift of Surrender Is Knowing Ourselves
Recognizing our true condition lets us know who we really are. I don't mean identifying all the trappings that make you enviable, like your shiny

new car, important job, or reputation at your church. Instead, surrender depends on knowing the real you beneath the carefully constructed facade. For most of us, that means acknowledging that we've got a lot of bags—the pain, stress, and heartache in life. We can't begin to acknowledge what we are using to manage our bags if we don't see what is really there. We have to learn to see and surrender to what is really there. But it is possible to see what is there and still decide that we can carry it ourselves, or that we must carry it ourselves. The process of self-knowledge leading to surrender is crucial, but it is a process that is easily circumvented. Seeing without surrender will always leave a gap between appearance and reality.

For example, I prided myself on all my self-knowledge. I was a therapist. I'd been in a counseling program famous for introspection. But now I saw my weakness. There was more appearance than reality. The self I had shown to the world was a public self, crafted with great care. Between my public self and my true experience lay a lot of baggage that I was unwilling to surrender. I thought I had to take everything I learned about myself and take care of it by myself. And that is where I got into trouble.

> Keep your eyes open…so you don't get musty and murky. Keep your life…well-lighted.
>
> —THE GOSPEL OF LUKE[2]

As we begin to consider the gift of surrender, I want to challenge you to think about some of your bags, to know yourself, and to recognize what you use to take care of your internal world.

PAIN

Maybe one of your bags is pain. The pain of being single. The pain of being married. Physical pain. Economic pain. Children—nothing can bring us pain like they do. Maybe you have pain from childhood abuse or neglect.

Researchers in the field of addiction suggest that over half of those who struggle with substance abuse have experienced some form of childhood trauma.[3] This can be a heavy, worn, and battered bag.

There can even be spiritual pain. In one of my favorite books, *Deep unto Deep,* Dana Candler describes a pain that I think most of us have experienced, if we're honest enough to admit it:

> All emotions seemed to sleep. One hour turned to two as I watched the clock almost minute by minute. This was one of the days when I could hardly remember the point of my focus. Why was I here? What was I doing? What was the point of the waiting? Have I missed it entirely? Is this all a waste? I moved from sitting to pacing, from reading to praying quietly and from praying quietly to silence. Still nothing. No response. No movement. No sound. Two hours turned to three. Morning turned to afternoon. And on and on the day went—slowly and painfully empty.[4]

DISFIGUREMENT

Perhaps you have a bag of disfigurement. Maybe it's the way you look, the way your life looks, or the way your family looks. I entered early adulthood with an ideal of how life ought to look. During the Christmas season of 2000, I spoke at a conference for college students ages eighteen to twenty-four. I introduced myself this way:

> I have a wonderful marriage. My husband serves me and cooks dinner, does the laundry, and has a fabulous job. We have two wonderful children with no real problems to speak of. They do well in school and would rather hang out with us than anyone. We probably have such a great life because we have a lot of money. We buy

everything we want and go everywhere we want, and everything turns out just like we hoped it would. I have a great job. I am a counselor and all of my clients are doing so well—but they keep coming back and paying me just because they like me. And I must say that I am happy with the way that I look. I love my body, my hair, and my wardrobe. All in all, life is just perfect.

I was speaking on the topic of perfectionism and trying to use irony to make a point. But I was shocked when these young people in my audience took my introduction as true! When I talked about my perfect marriage, they collectively sighed, "Ohhhh." And when I talked about my perfect children, once again they cooed, "Ahhhh." For a few minutes, I wanted to hide my bag rather than move into my real introduction. The truth was that my life had broken into pieces that I couldn't find a way to put back together again. My children were in middle and high school at the time, struggling with the shock of a broken family. In fact, I had gone to a parent-teacher conference to talk about a D that my son received on an essay in language arts, an essay that I wrote! I had to tell my audience that counseling is always hard work, and it was a difficult season at that time. I had recently lost two of my dear young clients to cancer. And I was, well, I was depressed, on the verge of a relapse. I knew the truth, I told them, and I now share this bag with you: the truth is that without imperfections and disfigurements, there is no story. Our imperfections link us. As soon as I acknowledged that Maria and the paroled convict were struggling with the same internal realities that I was—an inability to find something, or Someone, to carry their emotional baggage—I no longer felt separate from them. I stopped looking for differences and realized our similarities. No matter what addiction you or your family member struggles with, *we all suffer from the same condition.* We all have baggage that we desperately need help with.

SHAME

This is the bag that carries all the things wrong with us. Notice that I didn't say all the things that we've done wrong. That's the guilt bag! This is the shame bag. Ashamed that you're divorced, that you weren't asked to be a part of a certain group, that your car was made in the eighties, that you work in the mall.

A few years ago, I worked with a young woman who was struggling with a relational addiction. She could not be okay with herself unless she was in a romantic relationship with another woman. When she first came to see me, she was in such distress that she couldn't even speak. Finally, after several moments of silence, I inquired gently whether there was anything that she wanted to ask me.

She blurted out, "What about hell?"

"What about hell?" I asked, confused.

"Well, the last counselor told me that I was going to hell and that no one in the church would ever be in relationship with me again."

My heart broke for this young woman. She had been cruelly shamed by others in her faith. I wanted her to know the God whose name is Love. This God is present, right in her experience of shame, waiting for her to identify the Divine Presence, offering His companionship on the often difficult journey of being human.

The truth is that I believe God is found in every bag, even, and most especially, in the painful, tragic, and most humiliating things about us. God created us, so God's heart contains every conceivable human emotion. He feels more than we do. His heart contains *us,* no matter what is in our bags.

My bag of shame is a lot heavier than you might know by just looking at me. But I am learning that sitting with my shame in God's presence helps me see that God isn't shocked by it. In fact, He already seems to know about it, and He still accepts me.

SIN, WOUNDEDNESS, AND CONFUSION

And then there is another bag that seems pretty heavy, especially for those of us who struggle with addiction. Right now I will just speak for myself. I do things I don't want to do and seem incapable of doing the things I want to do. If I am honest, my motivations aren't as pure or noble as I wish they were. Over and over, my ability to be who I really want to be seems to be sabotaged by some inner agent over which I have no control. I hear television gurus proclaim that everything we need is within ourselves. I hope that isn't true. It surely isn't true for me. I echo what the Desert Fathers wrote, "Dust and ashes that I am. I love sin!" I'm in big trouble if I have to be the answer to this internal dilemma. Getting to the heart of this last addiction, Desert Father John Kolobos urged, "If you see someone going up to heaven by his own will, grab his leg and pull him down again."[5]

To be human is to be broken, carrying a bag whose weight bows us down at the core of our very being and keeps us from our original creation.

Of course, it's not all gloom and doom. There are bags filled with hope and dreams of beauty and family. There are bags filled with ideas and creativity. There are bags of giftedness, our unique gifts, even the eccentricities that are necessary parts of us.

We have a lot of bags.

BAGGAGE CARRIERS

Surrender did not come immediately for me in that drug and alcohol class. I was the one making a shopping list while the others were dutifully answering on their handouts the question "What are you carrying in your bags?" Then the group leader asked the pivotal question, "What are you using to carry all those bags?"

Of course I immediately identified addiction as a good baggage carrier. It initially promises to make everything seem lighter, less intense, less demanding. But I only had to recall my relapse and the panic of my friends and family to know that this baggage carrier only brought further chaos, conflict, and confusion into my life. Because I travel a lot, my mind did jump to real-life baggage, and I pictured myself carrying all my travel bags down the corridor of my local airport while I was under the influence. Arrest or disaster could follow. The real-world parallel confirmed to me the foolishness of believing that any addictive behavior—alcohol, working nonstop, people pleasing—could carry the emotional weight of my life.

There are other luggage carriers, ways in which we manage our emotional baggage. We've all tried conforming to certain rules and regulations. We resolve to deny or suppress our pain, disfigurement, shame, sin, and failure, determined to show only that which is presentable. We find ways to manage our bags. I think of addicts and their families who have made all kinds of rules for themselves:

- I will only drink on weekends.
- I won't eat after 6:00 p.m.
- I will make everyone like me.
- I won't say anything to her about her substance abuse.
- I will be really nice.
- I will only buy things that are on sale.
- I will be in only one relationship at a time.

This baggage carrier can look pretty good. I liken it to getting one of those three-dollar luggage carts at the airport and neatly organizing all your bags for transport. I did this once in the Orlando airport. I had a lot of bags. Right in the middle of the reception area, where larger-than-life

Mickey and Minnie grin down at you and crowds wait to greet happy people going to the Magic Kingdom, the zipper on my top bag broke, spilling my most private personal garments on the floor. The crowd was entertained, and I could almost hear Mickey laughing.

I thought I had my bags perfectly stacked; it's like trusting the baggage cart of rules. Eugene Peterson's translation in The Message poignantly points to the foolishness of using legalism and religious rule-keeping to manage our lives:

> We know very well that we are not set right with God by rule-keeping.... How do we know? We tried it—and we had the best system of rules the world has ever seen!... What actually took place is this: I tried keeping rules and working my head off to please God, and it didn't work.... Legalism is helpless.... For if any kind of rule-keeping had power to create life in us, we would certainly have gotten it by this time.[6]

If addiction and legalism can't carry the weight of our bags, there is one more luggage carrier that we seem to always fall back on: *We can do it ourselves.* This is the last addiction. Recently I met with an adolescent counseling client who was struggling at home and school, but having a hard time asking for help. One day, we actually packed real bags to represent all the bags that she was carrying; soon she had a big pile of suitcases and purses. I asked her how she thought she could manage all those bags. She thought for a while and said, "It would be hard, but I can carry them myself."

We loaded them up in the car and drove to Denver International Airport. We entered on the terminal level, and she managed to arrange all the bags so that she could carry them herself. With a little mischief in my voice, I said, "Okay, now let's go down the escalator." The fear in her eyes told me that she got it. She said, "I'm afraid I might break something."

My teenage client learned more quickly than most of us. We keep trying to manage our bags, but we can't do this by ourselves.

The Second Gift of Surrender Is Knowing That We Need Others

We can't need others (I mean really need them) and we can't give to others (I mean really bear their burdens and troublesome moral faults) unless we know that we are all broken. As we've looked at ourselves and our emotional baggage, did you notice how often the idea of something getting broken came up? All those bags break our backs, they break our hearts, and they break our spirits.

It is puzzling to me that the music, art, and books we like most are often direct expressions of human brokenness. The greatest human creativity testifies to our human weakness. Yet our response to our personal brokenness is that we need to hide it, keep it at arm's length, numb it with addiction, cover it up with self-righteousness, and certainly not burden anyone else with it.

Without surrender, we get caught in an impasse between high arrogance and low self-esteem, neither of which can work. High arrogance makes us believe that we can handle things, that others can't be trusted, and even that we do a better job of managing our lives than God does. Low self-esteem leads us to believe that we must handle things, because we'd be a burden to others or become unlovable if we revealed all of our baggage, and that even God eventually gets tired of our constant neediness.

Right before I left for Cambodia in 2005, I met with a client who comes from one of the wealthiest families in our community. We were talking about Christmas and my upcoming time in Cambodia. I asked her to describe the Christmas that she anticipated. It was filled with china, crystal, and extravagant gifts with beautiful wrappings. But she also told me that she was not speaking to her brother, her father wasn't speaking to her, and her mother would be very angry if any of the children spilled anything on the tablecloth. Her immediate family were actually practicing eating on a tablecloth at home, so that her children would not spoil the holiday festivities.

This woman had a lot of bags. But that wasn't the saddest part of the story. Certainly, the lovely gift bags were outweighed by the heavy bags of her broken family life. But the greatest tragedy to me was that she was trying to carry them all alone.

It was my trip to Cambodia that taught me another lesson about baggage, this time about the alternative of bearing one another's burdens. On that trip, we spent Christmas Eve in an orphanage in Anlong Veng. It was a hard day for me, hearing the stories of orphaned children. In their desperation to be loved, they clung to our legs and clamored for our attention. I wondered how I could simply get in the car and leave. We noticed that the children had painfully dry skin with many insect bites, because they had no screens on their windows. I ran for my suitcase to get my big bottle of Aveeno lotion. We began to rub the lotion on the children's arms and legs. My heart broke wide open as I watched the little boys rub lotion on their faces and run to the one mirror on the wall to look at themselves. They laughed with joy at their holiday treat. And then one of the children took the bottle, and they started rubbing lotion on one another's arms and legs. As they shared one another's burdens in the midst of their brokenness, I remembered the poorest family I knew—back in Denver, Colorado—who would be carrying all their bags that Christmas Day, beautiful designer bags, by themselves.

This is why I like Alcoholics Anonymous. We don't pretend we're not broken. We laugh and cry at our stories of human failures and foibles. I have a friend who attends meetings with me sometimes. She is not an alcoholic, but she often laments, "I wish I was an alcoholic or that there was some meeting for people whose lives have fallen apart without alcohol as their main problem." Somehow these meetings capture the mystery of our lives together; we help each other carry our bags.

Knowing ourselves—really knowing ourselves—and knowing that we need others are not the only gifts of surrender. Sometimes we can't see ourselves clearly, no matter how hard we try or how much psychoanalysis we pay for. Sometimes the human pyramid of support collapses, and things get even messier. People betray us, forget us, and let us down. Luggage is all over the place, like those airports with the four hundred thousand lost bags in December 2006.

The Final Gift of Surrender Is Knowing That We Need More
The Old Testament describes one more baggage carrier that goes beyond our human capacity:

> There was nothing attractive about him,
>> nothing to cause us to take a second look.
> He was looked down on and passed over,
>> a man who suffered, who knew pain firsthand.
> One look at him and people turned away.
>> We looked down on him, thought he was scum.
> But the fact is, it was *our* PAINS he carried—
>> *our* disfigurements, all the things wrong with *us*.
> We thought he brought it on himself,
>> that God was punishing him for his own failures.
> But it was our SINS that did that to him,
>> that ripped and tore and crushed him—*our sins*!
> He took the punishment, and that made us whole.
>> Through his bruises we get healed.
> We're all like sheep who've wandered off and gotten lost.

We've all done our own thing, gone our own way.
And GOD has piled all our [bags, every one of them],
   on him, on him.[7]

Christian biblical scholars believe that the prophet Isaiah was speaking of Jesus, the Son of God, coming to bear the weight of the world and bring healing. Other Old Testament scriptures prophesy of a sinless One who is coming to die and be resurrected for the sake of loving us. A recovering alcoholic, author Brennan Manning wrote of the difference this One might make: "If darkest night is upon you…, know that the risen Jesus is wild about you, even if you can't feel it. Listen beneath your pain for the voice of Abba God: 'Make ready for my Christ whose smile, like lightning, sets free the song of everlasting glory that now sleeps in your paper flesh like dynamite.'"[8]

Believer or unbeliever, perhaps you doubt that such a One can really make a difference, especially when it comes to addiction. After all, today He cannot be touched, seen, or heard from in the flesh, and it is in our flesh that we experience the cravings, withdrawal, pleasure, and pain of addiction. But I am coming to believe that I need something that is not of my flesh to save me. When it comes to salvation from real-life struggles, Saint Gregory of Nyssa expressed the need for spiritual over material, for mystery over science: "Concepts create idols; only wonder comprehends anything. People kill one another over idols. Wonder makes us fall to our knees."[9]

Shortly after college I lived in Winston-Salem, North Carolina. It was the home of a Moravian village that held a sunrise service every Easter. I didn't go to their service for the first two years I lived there. It seemed too early to get up, and I harbored some concerns that the Moravians might be a cult. The third year, I finally went to see what all the hoopla was about.

The whole town seemed to arrive in the field outside the village in the pitch black of early, early morning. Everyone was completely silent. And then at the first hint of sunrise, there was a majestic trumpet fanfare. I was not prepared for the echo that came next, as all the people turned to one another and repeated, "He is risen. He is risen. He is risen."

I recall vividly how tears streamed from my

> The God of curved space, the dry God, is not going to help us, but the son whose blood splattered the hem of his mother's robe.
>
> —JANE KENYON,
> *Bread and Wine: Readings for Lent and Easter*[10]

eyes at this surprise announcement of old news repeated anew. I remember thinking, *What if it's true?*

What if it's true? Then maybe we—headstrong, willful, heart-wrung, helpless addicts—maybe we can surrender.

PART II

TRUE STORIES
OF REDEMPTION

5

My Story: Wine and Other Spirits

> Making one's own wounds a source of healing,
> therefore, does not call for a sharing of superficial
> personal pains but for a constant willingness to see
> one's own pain and suffering as rising from the depth
> of the human condition which all men share.
> —Henri Nouwen, *The Wounded Healer*[1]

American culture abounds with confessional books, and I agree with those who criticize this glut of memoirs. It is easy to scorn people who go on *Dr. Phil* and spill shameful secrets, their own and those of their families, for millions of Americans to observe and for Dr. Phil to fix in just a few minutes. Why then, for what purpose, will I show myself and my long, terrible struggle with addiction? I want to expose my own addiction, not to revel in its dramatic qualities, but to tell you this: the door to redemption opens when we know that we all suffer from the same condition. At some core level we know that the boundaries between human beings are fluid. When I tell my story, I tell your story. This is why we read memoirs. Although I am a counselor and teacher who specializes in addiction, the border separating the healer from the hurting is blurry. When I weep for an alcoholic of the hopeless variety, I weep for me as well. I experience intimacy. I experience love. And that is why I tell my own story to you.

This chapter looks at the process of transformation in my own life and the role that addiction has played in that process. Yes, I am claiming that addiction actually contributes to transformation. I believe transformation is the means to reveal and to heal addiction. There is no doubt in my mind—whether it be the alcoholic who leaves a thirty-day treatment program and drives directly to the liquor store, or the overeater who weighs in at Weight Watchers and stops at Dunkin' Donuts on the way home— addiction is a wound. No one would *choose* the realities of addiction. It is a wound that has its roots in biology (genetics), environment, and use or behavior, but it is a wound.

And wounds are where Love gets in, and Love is the messenger of redemption.

The reality of addiction in our culture is evidenced by the number of books that come off the press every year on this subject. The difficulty of finding "the answer" to this agonizing problem is further shown by the statistics and stories of addicts that do not seem to be diminished by all of these books. Here are just a few of the books on my bookcase right now:

- *Under the Influence*
- *The Weight-Loss Diaries*
- *Diary of a Shopaholic*
- *Sober and Staying That Way*
- *The Language of Letting Go*
- *When Food Is Foe*
- *When Food Is Love*

- *Don't Call It Love*
- *Drinking: A Love Story*
- *Love Is a Choice*

The titles alone could fill this book. My bookcases reveal my own long-ing for a healing balm for this sometimes hideous and sometimes hidden wound of addiction. Anyone who knows me can attest to my earnest desire to solve my problems. My friends and family have watched me in the humiliation of detox and the hope of some new holistic program that infuses the brain with nutrients and amino acids. I have not ignored my wounds, but neither have I found the magic salve that works overnight, money back guaranteed.

As an addict and a woman who loves many addicts, I know that when we approach this subject, we are constantly in the tension of reformation versus transformation. Practically, we want the first. Spiritually, we long for the second. Just yesterday in my counseling office, I met with a woman whose experience reveals this tension. I have been seeing her for almost a year about her drinking—because her husband was worried about it. It took a few months for her to acknowledge that she is an alcoholic. Then it took a few more months of acknowledging the problems that alcohol was causing in her life for her to begin to try different means of addressing her problem. She finally settled on a combination of medication (Antabuse and antidepressants) and occasional meetings at a Twelve Step support group. Yesterday she reached across to give me a high-five.

She said, "I did it. I've gone thirty days without drinking!" She was in the midst of reformation; her behaviors were changing. And then she sighed.

"What's the sigh about?" I asked.

"It doesn't feel like anything in my life has really changed. I mean, my husband is happier, and I feel a little better physically, but I still feel restless and unhappy," she explained. She was thirsting for transformation. As is often the case, her reformed behaviors had now opened up a space in her soul, to wonder about *More*.

I have learned that transformation is a journey that has many steps. In this chapter, in the context of telling my own story, we are going to look at some of those necessary steps. Each one answers one of the debilitating beliefs in the life of an addict, which we examined in chapter 1: I am Crazy, I am Alone, I am Unforgivable, and I am Hopeless. As I share my own experiences of addiction and redemption, you will note that progress for me has not been linear, not perfect. It has been a halting few steps forward and a few steps back. I am on a journey toward greater self-awareness and the redeeming truth that my wounds are where Love gets in. It's a journey that I wouldn't trade for all the world.

UNDERSTANDING IN THE MIDST OF CRAZINESS

Understanding answers the addict's fear, "I am crazy." There are two components to understanding that make it complete. First, we must face reality. For family members this can be frustrating, because reality seems all too obvious to us. Part of the insidious nature of addiction is that it hides itself from the very person who needs healing. Second, we must receive compassion. Reality without compassion will only result in self-contempt, which will continue to fuel addiction. Compassion without reality will result in self-delusion, which will fuel denial.

Facing Reality

Addiction and delusion go hand in hand. In order to explain the craziness of addictive behaviors, reality must be faced squarely. It is a mystery to me how this occurs. It might surprise you to hear that I don't believe consequences make us face reality. In fact, one of the most baffling components of an addiction is why someone would continue to do the same things in the face of such dire consequences. We often talk about people "hitting bottom" and finally acknowledging their addiction. We addicts know that there is no bottom. In spite of previous consequences, we can always risk or justify one more go at our addiction.

When I first acknowledged my alcoholism, I hadn't experienced a lot of consequences. I was mostly afraid of what might be happening to me as I watched my intake of alcohol increase and began to experience some physical symptoms of tolerance and withdrawal. My underlying addiction to "doing it all right," which included approval seeking, looking good, and a fear of rejection, was not even on my radar. In response to my failure when it came to drinking, my other addiction went into high gear. All of my energy was turned outward in my need to appear perfect, or least pretty good. Inside I felt increasingly isolated, alienated, and alone. Even though I wasn't drinking, I felt as if I were living a double life. My outside didn't match my inside, and I was afraid that no one could see the inside and remain in relationship with me.

> It's your life that must change, not your skin.... What counts is your life.
>
> —THE GOSPEL OF LUKE[2]

When I relapsed shortly after my marriage broke apart, it became increasingly difficult for me to hide everything that was inside. The relapse revealed to others and to me that I didn't have it all together. Slowly, I began to face reality:

- I am an alcoholic.
- I can't rely on alcohol to numb or soothe my pain.
- I can't escape my life.
- I am not perfect.
- I can't change the past.
- I can't rely on the approval of others.

- My failed marriage didn't make me feel loved.
- I have wasted time seeking the approval of others.
- The approval of others doesn't fill my emptiness.

As these truths began to penetrate my mind and heart, I gained the ability to see the reality of my addictions, the reality of my misery, and the reality of my relationships.

It didn't take long for me to notice the reality of my alcoholism. In just one day, I was back to drinking more and more to get the desired result. There was no starting over with alcohol for me. I had spent years, though, hiding my relapse from most people and hiding the reality of my other addiction (to people pleasing) from myself.

In her memoir about her own alcoholism, *Note Found in a Bottle,* Susan Cheever wrote about the cunning distortion of alcoholism:

> Even these days when everyone thinks they know about alcoholism,
> it still hides. No one imagines that their own drinking is a problem.
> No one guesses that young people, people whose faces aren't red,
> whose bodies aren't bloated, who don't stumble and slur, might still
> be completely controlled by their drinking. Alcohol warps the mind
> long before it even begins on the body—that's why we love it so.[3]

If alcoholism can be hidden for a time, people pleasing and the toll it takes on the addict can be hidden for a lifetime. When we use others to rip off a little self-esteem by "using" their approval to feel better about ourselves or to quench a bit of our neediness, we can go unnoticed. We can even look good, but as with substance abuse, these behaviors can run our lives and become completely disorienting. It is crazy-making to be in your own mind and someone else's at the same time! This addiction, too, is a wound rooted in biology (personality type), environment (often parental aloofness or rejection), and behaviors (like agreeing to something that violates your integrity in order to make people like you). The more people pleasing controls your inner world, the less you know yourself and the less you act in accordance with your true desires and values.

The misery that results from addiction is almost impossible to describe. We can certainly list the external costs—job loss, physical symptoms, legal consequences, relational distress—but the internal costs are harder to measure. How do you quantify self-hatred, loss of self-confidence, lack of self-control, diminishing self-respect? Notice all the damage to self in these miseries. The idea that self must fix this broken self is self-defeating. But I sure kept trying to fix myself with myself. I was determined not only to not drink, but to be a compassionate, wise, mature, grateful, and self-confident woman. I awoke many mornings afraid to look at myself in the mirror, afraid that what would peer back would grotesquely reveal my broken inner self and my helplessness to fix me. Thank God, whose grace can break through regardless of our intent.

Transformation occurs in our willingness to continue facing the truth of who we are, regardless of how threatening or unpleasant the reality might be. It means hanging in there, learning our own mind tricks and how they defeat us, recognizing our avoidances, acknowledging our lapses, and finally, learning that we cannot handle ourselves.

Receiving Compassion

Most addicts don't fear pain. We prove that over and over again as we stumble into some pretty harsh consequences. Instead, we fear comfort. To be comforted requires that we be vulnerable, that we trust someone to see us and love us. Denial keeps us trapped: I can't admit reality, so I can't receive grace.

Redemption begins to penetrate the hard ground of addiction when we can risk telling the truth about our lives. Facing reality risks hoping and/or trusting that God and others are good. Receiving compassion risks hoping and/or trusting that I am good. These can seem like enormous risks when we have been hurt, disappointed, or betrayed by others and when we have hurt, disappointed, and betrayed as well. However, if we don't take these risks, we are left with only ourselves, a recipe for disaster for addicts.

I knew that taking off my addictive armor of people pleasing had to begin with telling the truth about my life. I braced myself. One or two close friends and family knew about my relapse. No one knew about my continued struggle with perfectionism, people pleasing, and hiding my interior life in hopes that others would love me. I began to see a counselor, a wise white-haired older man who offered me more compassion than I could bear. He felt pity for my woundedness and secret struggles. He helped me untangle the roots of my addictions and put words to my self-destructive behaviors. He never lectured or shook his head in disgust. He held out comfort even when I closed my hands to his gift. He was the first to help me confront the second belief of the addict: I am alone.

> Be patient with everyone but above all with yourself; I mean, don't be disturbed about your imperfections… There's no better way of growing…in the spiritual life than to be always starting over again.…
>
> —St. Francis de Sales[4]

COMMUNITY IN THE MIDST OF ISOLATION

Authentic community begins to dismantle the addict's belief, "I am alone." Emotional recovery can take place only within community, because there we discover just how inextricably linked we are to one another, how much we influence one another, and how much our willingness to tell the truth, to feel pain, and to express joy helps others to do the same. I certainly experienced this in Alcoholics Anonymous. This was one gift of my relapse after my marriage fell apart—my regular participation in AA. However, after the relapse I harbored the suspicion that other people in my life would not be so understanding or accepting, and so in the rest of my life I worked really hard to prove that the "bad" part of me (the alcoholic) was not that strong. What I didn't realize is that this people-pleasing, proving-I'm-good part of me was just as destructive as the active alcoholic. Separating these parts of myself was keeping me from living with integrity.

One gift of facing reality is that it eventually becomes too much work to keep up appearances. I got tired! Then my close friends and my counselor dared me to take a bigger risk. I was already scheduled to speak at my church retreat, and now I struggled with extreme anxiety. I wanted to tell the truth about my life, but I was afraid of embarrassing those who asked me to speak, and myself. Finally, the weight of my reality collapsed my resolve to hide, and I sent an e-mail to the man I was scheduled to speak with. He is a respected teacher and counselor in our community. I told him the truth and waited with a mixture of dread and anticipation for his response. It felt good to not hide, but I was frightened that he would back out of the retreat.

His e-mail finally came:

I hear fear in your words. Fear that you have finally done something
that will push everyone away and prove that you are not lovable.
I recognize the fear, because I often struggle with the same anxiety.
I think that you and I should speak about the power of Love to
banish this fear. It just might change people's lives.

I couldn't stop reading his words, over and over. They thrilled me and scared me. It seemed too good to be true that others would know me and still want me, that my failure would not exclude me from relationships, and that my imperfections actually made real relationships possible. I was just beginning to understand the truth of redemption; it enters with Love, and love is felt most profoundly in the midst of our wounds.

When I received compassion, not only from my friend, but then overwhelmingly from my church community after I shared my story at the retreat, I was able to respond to the realities that I had acknowledged earlier:

I am an alcoholic.

I am living with integrity.

I can't rely on alcohol to numb or soothe my pain.

I can rely on myself, others, and God.

I can't escape my life.

I can live in a life that I don't need to escape from.

I am not perfect.

I don't have to be perfect to be loved.

I can't change the past.

The past can be remembered redemptively.

I can't rely on the approval of others.

I don't need the approval of others to know that I am loved.

My failed marriage didn't make me feel loved.

I can mourn the loss and feel loved by others.

I have wasted time seeking the approval of others.

I don't have to do that anymore.

The approval of others doesn't fill my emptiness.
There is room for authentic relationships now.

I have discovered that the single force that keeps most people in their addictive behaviors is hiding. God's first story about human beings describes this energy in Genesis 3:7–8: "And the eyes of them both were opened, and they knew that they were naked; and they sewed fig leaves together, and made themselves aprons. And they heard the voice of the LORD God walking in the garden in the cool of the day: and Adam and his wife hid themselves from the presence of the LORD God amongst the trees of the garden" (KJV).

We do all kinds of crazy things to stay in hiding, not believing that we can disclose our wounds and find healing love. It is a real risk to come out of hiding; not every story ends with a wonderful e-mail like the one that I got. Sadly, some people may reject or even mock you. But if you believe that you need a human being who will completely understand you, forgive you, and meet your needs, then you will find plenty of reasons to go back to hiding. The only reality that allows us to risk trusting that others are good is knowing that there is a Greater Good that we can return to in the midst of disappointment and human failure.

FORGIVENESS IN THE MIDST OF SHAME

The experience of being forgiven pulls us out of the stagnating mire of a self-centered focus on our pain and confronts the cry of addiction, "I am unforgivable." What keeps us from seeking a forgiveness outside of ourselves, from believing in a God who lives and loves to forgive, from offering our brokenness to Another who can heal? I believe it is that we hate our woundedness—we do not see it as a gift.

Addiction shatters not only our dreams for ourselves or our family members, it shatters us. We lose the ideals for our lives, but worse, we find in the core of our beings that something about *us* is broken. Even though this is extremely humbling and disorienting, one gift of addiction is experiencing the end of ourselves. In the rubble of our dreams for our relationships, our health, our reputations, and our competence, we come face to face with the reality that *we* are the broken dreams. And it is through the cracks of this brokenness that God can dream *His* dream.

This is His dream: "It started when God said, 'Light up the darkness!' and our lives filled up with light." God longs to make the dark places light, so "God has chosen the foolish…of the world," and "we have this treasure in earthen vessels, so that the surpassing greatness of the power will be of God and not from ourselves."[4]

It is hard to believe that redemption comes in addiction, light in darkness, wholeness in brokenness, and healing in woundedness—unless you have a story greater than your own to go by. I can know my story and face its reality, but if my story is all that I have, then I will get bogged down again in my determination to try again, do it better, and save myself. It's the last addiction.

A few years ago I attended a passion play at a local inner-city church. This production obviously didn't have a big budget. The garden of Gethsemane consisted of large plastic trees with strips of black plastic trash bags hanging down. The man who played John (the one described in Scripture as the disciple Jesus loved) was developmentally disabled, and he kept wringing his hands through the play and saying, "Oh my, oh my," in a nervous voice. When the man portraying Jesus walked up the aisle of the church carrying his cross, you could see the makeup of his wound peeling away from his back. I kept saying to myself, "This is ridiculous." The humble passion play, far from any Hollywood version of this story, reminded me of the complete leap of faith required to believe that this story could make a difference in my life.

I can't explain how it happened, but by the end of the production I had forgotten about the trash-bag trees and the bad costuming. I began to think about the mess of my life, a good church woman addicted to alcohol, work, people pleasing, and probably a few more things. My initial contempt for the poorly done play reminded me of my lifetime certainty that no one was strong enough, smart enough, or open hearted enough to "handle" me. I knew, heart and soul, that I needed a story bigger than I. I was desperate for a story that could not be contained in a human production. I needed a story that could contain me.

I walked out of the church saying, "This is a ridiculous story, but it is *my* story." I saw that I needed a love so demonstrative that I couldn't miss it. I needed Someone who would surrender His strength and offer a sacrifice of love, Someone the opposite of me. Someone wounded for me— beaten, molested, and abused.

The play brought it home: Jesus surrendered His strength, and at the ninth hour of the following day, as He hung naked, nailed to the cross, He said, "Father, forgive them; for they know not what they do."[5] *For they know not what they do.* If there ever was a phrase that described addiction, this was it. And I believe in this story God is saying, "I give you My Son, My sacrifice, *My deepest wound* to forgive and heal your deepest wound." Our wounds need His wound. We are joined in our wounds.

When I surrender my wounds to His death on the cross for me, I am acknowledging that I can't save myself. This concept of surrender is more foreign that we might think, especially if we are familiar with words of faith. We can believe that Jesus died, was buried, and arose again. We can say the words, "I know Jesus died for my sins. I want Him to come into my heart." But surrender goes further. Surrender is joined to belief when I *know* that I am utterly helpless, and I exchange my ways of being good, of proving myself, of pulling myself up by my bootstraps, for The Way of needing Jesus's love, forgiveness, mercy, grace, and holiness as much as I need oxygen. This desperation is only born out of dying to myself.

Whether it is addiction or another excruciating reality of life that strikes the final wound that leads to surrender, it becomes a gift when we invite the healing wounds of Jesus to minister to our wounds.

HARD WORK IN THE MIDST OF HOPELESSNESS

I don't know any other way to say it. To confront an addiction redemptively is hard work. It's not all mystery and mysticism. It involves beginning again, trying again, hoping again, and believing again. In *Addiction and Grace,* Gerald May says it this way: "Addiction cannot be defeated by the human will acting on its own, nor by the human will opting out and turning everything over to divine will. Instead, *the power of grace flows most fully when human will chooses to act in harmony with divine will.*"[6]

Whether it is attending a Twelve Step meeting, seeking the advice of a physician, asking for help from family, or telling the truth about our lives to a trusted friend, we must choose, again and again, something higher than the default mode of our addictions. We get into trouble by hoping that whatever we choose is The Solution rather than surrendering to the journey of transformation, the journey of choosing again and again. The struggle will not end, but each battle comes with another invitation to redemption, which makes the struggle redemptive in itself.

Perhaps you are feeling frustrated as you read, on your own behalf or on the behalf of an addicted family member. You may be wondering, "But when is she going to tell us what to *do?*" My answer is, "Do everything—everything that you can think of, that you read about or hear suggested by well-meaning friends." One of my favorite sentences in the "Big Book" of

Alcoholics Anonymous is "If you have decided you want what we have and *are willing to go to any length to get it*—then you are ready to take certain steps"[7] (emphasis added). As the Alcoholics Anonymous slogan suggests, "It all works, if you work it"; however, the work itself is not our savior. In this hard work we must stay open to something outside of ourselves; eventually we will have to surrender to that something; we'll have to give in to it as completely as we once did to our central activity. It must become what we think about when we wake up in the morning, what we plan for, what we talk about, what we give our time and energy to, what becomes the momentum of our lives.

What this means practically in the lives of different addicts is the subject of the rest of this book. For me that something is giving and receiving love. It has not always been very practical. I am prone to isolate and rely on myself to deal with myself. And then something happens—sometimes it's falling flat on my face and sometimes it's an unexpected encounter with another person—that reminds me that apart from Love, I will wander on my own from one idol to another, "trad[ing] the glory of God who holds the whole world in his hands for cheap figurines you can buy at any roadside stand."[8] When I read and learn of God's love for me, when I remember that my central activity must be giving and receiving love, then something in my spirit leaps toward it. Something in my heart is freed when I receive love, no matter how good or bad I am. Something in my will is checked and balanced when I evaluate my choices through the grid of giving and receiving love.

Several months ago I was meeting with the wise counselor I mentioned earlier. I had come to love him and to respect and value his insights and advice. In this particular session he asked me to imagine "drunk Sharon" sitting in an empty chair. My task was to talk to her. I immediately felt a tinge of shame and some compassion.

I began, "I know you don't want to be in this condition right now,

Sharon. I understand that you're trying to escape yourself and your pain, and you foolishly thought that you could handle things, but you can't. I know you want more than anything else to be free—free to feel and love and be yourself with others…"

My counselor interrupted me. "You're speaking as if you were 'drunk Sharon.'"

I didn't see what he was talking about.

"What does 'drunk Sharon' really want?" he asked. Every time he used the phrase "drunk Sharon," I cringed. I felt shame and embarrassment, and I wanted more and more to hide this part of me from the rest of the world.

I tried to ignore my shame and answer his question. "I guess she wants love and acceptance, no matter what."

His eyes shone with warmth. "Yes, that is why *I* love 'drunk Sharon.'"

I looked at him for several minutes. I couldn't believe what he was saying. Didn't he understand? This was the weak, despicable part of me that needed to be punished and hidden. But I couldn't dismiss the love in his eyes. It was as if my reality, my aloneness, my shameful behavior, and my hopelessness (all the evidences of my addiction) had run into something stronger—Love. Rainer Maria Rilke wrote, "Everything terrifying is, in its deepest being, something helpless that wants our help."[9] Perhaps the only self-help that means anything is receiving love. And perhaps that means everything.

6

DAVID'S STORY: SEX APPEAL

The key to our sexual healing, the key to all healing
is to surrender our shame to the Lover of our souls.
—PETER HIETT[1]

D avid, a well-respected professional, came to see me for counseling
when his twenty-year marriage was falling apart. Over thirty-five
years of secrets were starting to slither through the cracks of his marriage.
His wife had learned of an affair, which opened the door to David's confessing more than ten affairs in twenty years of marriage, which prompted
David to examine for the first time the years of childhood sexual abuse that
he had suffered.

Sex addicts are confusing to many of us and enraging to others. What
would make a successful man, one who loved his wife and children, engage
in such outlandish serial infidelity? What would make a respected busi-
nesswoman, a committed mother, masturbate five to six hours every day?
Why would an upstanding man in his community walk behind a local
business and expose himself? Are these just sick people who can't control
their private parts? This chapter concerns the way our private parts are connected to our hearts. When that connection is misunderstood, abused, or
violated, a cavern is carved into our souls, setting off a craving that feels

insatiable. I will tell you David's story of self-discovery, self-disclosure, and self-abandonment. David found himself to lose himself, and his is an amazing story of redemption.

SEXUAL ADDICTION DEFINED

Sexual addiction may be difficult to define in a day when pornography is touted as every man's battle and its use is sometimes even encouraged to "spice up" marriage. In America, we spend more on pornography in one year than the annual sales of Coca-Cola, and almost two-thirds of all visits and commerce on the Internet involve a sexual purpose.[2]

Unlike substance abuse, a problematic relationship with a mood-altering substance, sexual addiction is a problematic relationship with a mood-altering experience. For the sexual addict, pornography, sexual chat rooms, engaging in sexual encounters, or almost any sexual activity becomes increasingly important, taking over the person's time, other priorities, and relationships. Like a drug addict, the sex addict becomes less and less interested in the real relationships and experiences that make up a healthy life.

In biological fact, sex addicts are drug addicted. Rather than introducing an external source, like drugs or alcohol, to change brain chemistry, they have found a way to induce the chemical release of certain brain chemicals within their own systems. As with other addictions, there is a pattern of out-of-control behavior, an inability to stop despite adverse consequences, and a need for escalating sexual experiences to achieve the desired high. The question is not how many affairs you must have or how many Internet sites you must visit before you are a sex addict. These questions parallel the question of how many drinks it takes to make you an alcoholic. The right question concerns not quantity but pattern. Once an alcoholic takes a drink or a sex addict begins to fantasize or surf the Web, the behaviors take on lives of their own.

One of my friends, a fellow counselor, explains that a childhood experience led to his pattern of behavior:

> As a young boy I was regularly exposed to pornography. At a time when my childhood passions should have been directed toward stuffed animals and superheroes, my heart and mind became obsessed with erotic images. Lust became my preoccupation and shame became my identity. For nearly three decades I lived in a secret prison. But after years of lying to myself and to others, I was "found out" and healing could finally begin.[3]

Sexual addictions are connected to relational addictions, which might not have an overtly sexual component. Flirting, emotional bonding, and fantasizing about romantic entanglements can be addictive as well. Men and women who are needy and are looking for other people to make them feel whole are particularly vulnerable to relational addictions. As in other addictions, the addict seeks a pleasurable high or focus that temporarily obliterates all problems. These behaviors and obsessions can have the same costs as any addiction—eroding other relationships, consuming time, and kidnapping the heart and soul. Any of these central activities can destructively impact family, career, ministry, health, and finances.

Even in nonsexual relational addictions, the flirting and fantasy release naturally occurring endorphins in the brain that result in a high. Some researchers suggest that these electrochemical interactions in the brain parallel the molecular structure of morphine *but are many times more powerful.* Researchers have studied rats that are habituated to morphine or heroin and have learned that the rats will go through pain in order to obtain more of the drug. The scientists then discovered that the rats would endure even more pain to receive sexual stimulation than they endured merely to receive the drugs.[4] Ask any man who has decided he will no longer surf the Internet for pornographic Web sites or a woman who has begun obsessing about an office romance, "How easy is it to just stop?" The momentum of addiction has hijacked the heart and mind, just as it does in substance abuse. But there is a difference in sexual addictions. Sexuality is not merely something that we do, it is part of who we are. So when sexual addiction becomes the central activity, trying to change that behavior feels like cutting off a part of yourself.

Ask David. For all of his adult life, he had been constantly engaged in some sort of hidden and forbidden relationship. When he began counseling, he had been caught by his wife in one affair. What she didn't know was that he was simultaneously engaging in two more affairs and had a history of serial affairs throughout their marriage.

Understanding in the Midst of Craziness

David's wife certainly didn't understand what was going on, and David didn't either. To begin to speak the truth of his sexual addiction seemed to him like opening a door to such disgusting darkness that no one could bear to look at it. In his wonderful project dedicated to sexual addiction, lyricist and musician Steve Siler describes the fears of a man caught in sexual addiction:

> I'm in the church on Sunday morning
> Got the family and the new SUV
> Your co-worker and your neighbor
> I'm exactly who you think I should be
> But my eyes feast where none can see
> On visual profanity

I'm a traitor

A betrayer

A double minded-man

I'm a liar

A decay-er of everything I stand for

A voyeur in the dark

An adulterer of the heart

A betrayer

A traitor…

I feel like I'm drowning

Out of control

Like an addict who needs a fix

Selling my soul for the counterfeit high

In these pictures and pixels

God, I want to pray to you

But it feels like you wouldn't want me to.[5]

David soon acknowledged that he was an addict, using fantasy, flirting, risk-taking behaviors, and sexual encounters in a repetitive, degenerative, and eventually unmanageable fashion. He knew that he was trying to medicate something, but as is often the case in addiction, he was so consumed with the intricacies and shame of his behaviors that he didn't think about *why* he was stuck in such a destructive pattern.

As David and I began talking about his childhood, never-before-told stories of patterns of sexual abuse came out. When he was about eight years old, David participated in a recreational sports program in his community. The leader of the program was a charismatic, fun young man. At the end of every day of activity, the leader picked one child to sit on his lap while he told stories to the others. Everyone wanted to be the favorite. David learned about all that went with being the leader's favorite the day that he got picked. While sitting on the leader's lap, covered by a blanket, he was sexually abused.

As an eight-year-old, David did not have the capacity to understand this hidden, physically arousing, and confusing experience of being chosen. He never told anyone about the experience. The pain that David recalled most vividly was that he was never chosen to be the favorite again. He wondered why, what he had done wrong, and what he could do to gain the attention of the leader again. He recalled being a few years older and hearing his mother talk about a sports coach that had been arrested for sexually abusing some of his players. His mother talked with disgust about the coach and his victims. David knew that he would never tell his mother what had happened to him.

From that time on, these themes were woven into David's life, the themes of hiding, sexualizing otherwise nonsexual relationships, and being good enough to be chosen. David carried a weight of shame that he believed could be alleviated only in the thrill of a new, clandestine relationship. As David talked about his life, past and present, his shame was palpable. He sat on my couch with shoulders slumped. He rarely made eye contact.

> What we do know...about child abuse [is that]...some of these children grow up impelled chiefly to contain rather than repeat the trauma.... They act as if they were psychologically healthy, presenting a facade of normality that covers an essential hollowness of soul.
>
> —Leonard Shengold, MD, *Soul Murder*[6]

It was as if a three-hundred-pound gorilla was on his back, constantly demanding his attention.

The Gift of Shame

Shame could be called a violation of the self, exposing the self as foolish. Guilt says, "I have done something wrong." Shame says, "I am wrong. I am a fool."

What do you say to someone who is steeped in shame? What do you say to a man who believes that he has responded to being sexually abused by becoming a monstrous perpetrator of hurt and harm against his own family? If I said to David, "I assure you that you're not *that* bad," the words would have only bounced off his armor of shame.

Nevertheless, shame can become a gift. It can reveal something that is core to the soul; it can expose a part of us that has foolishly aligned ourselves to a god that is not God. I knew that healing could not begin for David unless he could see that he had trusted a pattern of behavior that was violating the good intent of relationships and that was violating him so that neither he nor his relationships were what they were intended to be.

All addiction comes from trusting something or someone, making that central activity god, and discovering that we violate it and it violates us. This discovery is debilitating and horrendous. Philosopher Jean-Paul Sartre calls it the "hemorrhaging of the soul." There is no experience so awful as shame, and yet it seems that the addict chooses a pattern of behavior that only intensifies shame. Why? Understanding the answer to this question can actually transform shame from a curse into a gift.

In shame there is relief from the desire for intimacy. When I am nothing but a failure, when my inner life must be hidden from everyone because it is too dark and dangerous, and when my behaviors are unspeakable and inexplicable, then I am not worthy of true intimacy. This is the trap of addiction. Addiction initially sends us into a pattern of living that promises relief from the pain and sorrow of relationships, and then it seals our fate by guaranteeing that no one would want to be in relationship with us if they really knew us.

When David was sexually abused, part of the insidious reality of the abuse was that it awakened something good in him: a desire to be chosen, to be close, and to be touched. Tragically, all of these good things were stirred up in the context of something perverted and evil. As a child, David did not have the capacity to sort this out, and because he was isolated from others with this story and in much of his life, all of these desires went underground. His normal desires were distorted into choices that promised elements of what he was made for, but in a pattern of behavior that guaranteed he would not get what he really wanted.

Understanding this process allowed David to identify his addiction and all of its ensuing shame, which brought to the surface a gift of understanding in the midst of all this tragedy—a commitment to love *and* not love. David began to understand that even as a child, he was full of passion that he didn't know what to do with. His mother made him believe that his questions, exuberance, and emotions were a burden, or even disgusting. His father was consumed with work and was never available. He did not play with David, pay attention to David's accomplishments or needs, or express any curiosity about David's life. After his experience of sexual abuse had aroused passion in David, it went unexplained except for the shame of his mother's comments. David concluded that passion, really anything connected with relational life, only resulted in shame or dismissal. The problem was that the passion for relational connection did not go away. David learned to channel that passion into underground relationships that would make him feel in control and keep his desires out of the light, where they risked rejection or refusal. His bondage to illicit relationships left little passion for legitimate relationships. Addiction has the effect of consuming true passion and shutting you down.

If you or someone you love is struggling with sexual addiction, the greatest gift you can receive or offer is to look for what is beneath that great weight of shame. It might surprise you to learn that one study of men who were sexually addicted revealed that beneath this addiction was a desire for real relationships. Two groups, the addicted men and men who didn't struggle with sexual compulsion, were shown pornographic images. The researchers discovered that the men who acknowledged a struggle with sexual addiction spent most of their time looking at the women's eyes, while the other men did not focus on any specific area of the image. The addicts' focus on the eyes gives a clue as to what they were really seeking. Although they got lured by the body parts in the pornographic images, their focus on the eyes suggests wanting to find a real woman behind the unreal image.

We were created to be in relationships, so the soul was created to be in motion—active—with respect to passion. Remember, addiction is momentum that kidnaps the brain and stops the motion of the soul. We were designed to be searching, seeking, knocking, and constantly moving toward that for which we were made. Addiction shuts down passion and kills the soul.

Slowly, David began to confront that gorilla that was on his back. He acknowledged that what he really wanted was good, but he was trying to fill himself with what he didn't really need (extramarital affairs) in order to distract himself from what he wanted most but didn't feel competent to handle.

David and his wife set out on the long, long journey of looking at their relationship and seeking true intimacy. This book cannot tell all of the ups and downs that they encountered during the next few years. This was tough work. There were bad days when David's wife was overwhelmed by learning of his affairs and the details of how she had been betrayed. David learned to go to his wife on these days and on good days too, and to not avoid the subject or hide. He has said to his wife thousands of times, "I know that I hurt you terribly, and I don't want to ever do that again." His simple acknowledgment of the pain he caused and what he desires in their relationship reminds him of what he really wants—intimacy with his wife—and his determination to do the long, hard work of a real, growing relationship.

COMMUNITY IN THE MIDST OF ISOLATION

David didn't have friends. He had co-workers and acquaintances that he might go for a bike ride with, but no one really knew him. As David and his wife journeyed along the difficult path of transforming their relationship, it became apparent that David needed other companions. He got discouraged. He got angry. He felt ashamed. And his old pattern of behavior still beckoned him, with the promise of relief from everything that he was in the midst of. I encouraged David to find a group of men who might understand what he was going through. David didn't believe that there was such a group. He still suspected that his addiction was so dark and dangerous that no one would be able to understand him. The "tapes" of his mother's expressions of dismay and disgust still played in his head.

Though he doubted, David was willing to do whatever I suggested. Real relationships and healing in his family had become his reward, far more meaningful and sweeter than any secret affair might be. He attended a new men's group in our area, beginning with a weekend retreat. When David returned from this retreat, I knew that something had happened. He sat up straight on my couch. He looked me right in the eyes as he talked. The gorilla was gone.

David told me of a weekend like nothing he had ever experienced before. All the men told their life stories. David explained that he waited to go last, still fearing that his story was the worst. However, as he heard the other men's stories of addiction, he realized that they all suffered from the same condition. They all wanted meaningful relationships and had been ensnared by behaviors that kept them out of the very relationships they really wanted.

When David started to tell his story, he began to weep. He kept on crying the whole time he talked. When he finished, the other men were silent for several minutes. David said he feared that he had been too much for them. And then one by one, the men got up from the circle and came and hugged David. Much to his surprise, these men hadn't heard how different David was, but how much they had in common. They became a band of brothers that day, and they remain friends today. David often says, "If I'm even tempted to go back to my old way of life, there are seven men that I could call right now who would be there for me."

Recently David came to one of my classes on addiction to tell his story. He explained the healing power of community this way: "I still have a long way to go, but I'm not doing it alone anymore." His statement reminded me that the very experiences that we think will make us rejected by others are often the links to relationships and to further healing.

A woman in my Alcoholics Anonymous group often tells the story of her son, who was born with muscular dystrophy. Despite regular physical therapy and assurances from doctors that he could walk, my friend's son would not even try to walk on his own. By age six he was still completely wheelchair bound. Sad and discouraged, my friend registered her son for a week-long camp in the mountains, a camp just for children with muscular dystrophy. On the last night of the camp, all of the children sat around a campfire with their parents. Midway through the campfire ceremony,

> "Hallo...I've found somebody just like me. I thought I was the only one of them."
>
> —A. A. MILNE, *Winnie-the-Pooh*[7]

much to my friend's surprise and delight, her son stood up, took a few halting steps to throw a branch on the fire, and walked back to his chair.

"How did you start walking by yourself?" she asked with joy.

"I didn't know that I could, until I saw other people like me," he explained.

The value of community for those struggling with addiction cannot be overstated. When we see others like us, walking, taking steps toward a new way of living, we begin to believe in redemption—for people like us.

FORGIVENESS IN THE MIDST OF SHAME

David often found himself vulnerable to the trap of the final addiction. Like many addicts, as he began to make amends for the ways he had harmed others, he found, welling up within, a resolve to be better than ever. Making amends and resolving to do better are not bad things, but when they become central to recovery, they can fuel an addiction just as deadly as the first addiction. When I am responsible for my own forgiveness—by being appropriately sorry and being consistently good—I become addicted to myself. I become my own god. And when I become my own god, I am in trouble.

The process of becoming unstuck from a central activity requires tremendous bravery, because we're completely changing our way of perceiving reality. We are changing the frequently traveled pathways of our brains and also the programming of our souls. Becoming who God intended us to be is the type of redemption that I long for and want for my friends and clients. I don't think that means people with ironclad wills, whiter teeth, weed-free yards, and strife-free lives—people without embarrassment, failures, and disappointments and living happily ever after. Pursuing this ideal chains us to ourselves. We become committed to a program of self-help that is reliant upon self alone.

Redemption occurs when we are in a process of self-abandonment that is reliant upon a Power greater than ourselves. By self-abandonment I don't mean ignoring our stories, our needs, or our desires. I mean knowing that our stories, our needs, and our desires must connect with Someone other than ourselves.

David was a hard worker. In therapy, he did everything that I suggested might be helpful. He was disciplined and committed to a new way of life. And he struggled with depression. Some days were so dark he could barely get out of bed, days when the ghosts of the past slithered in and brought back his weaknesses and failures. I reminded David that he had done great work on his own story, but that he still needed to connect his story to a Greater Story.

David and his family attended church regularly. David had begun reading his Bible every day, but he explained to me, "It doesn't seem personal. I don't know why, but it isn't doing anything for me." I didn't have five foolproof steps that David could follow to *feel* connected spiritually. I simply encouraged him to keep on. He didn't need to find God (that's part of the last addiction—that we can do it ourselves!), but he needed to be open to God finding him.

If that sounds simple to you, then you might not understand what "being open" means. Being open means that you keep showing up, keep listening, keep reading and meditating, even if there seems to be no answer. For those of us who struggle with addiction, that seems crazy. Why be open to a God who admits that to Him a "day is like a thousand years"?[8] We addicts are all too quick and good at finding something or someone that works much more predictably and immediately.

I will never forget the session when David told me about God's finding him. David had attended his regular church service. David's church was pretty formal and cerebral in its message. David liked the regular pastor's preaching. He explained to me that it "encouraged him to think." David didn't know that what he really needed was encouragement to feel. That day, a special speaker concluded the service a little differently than the regular minister. Anyone who wanted extra prayer was invited to come to the front of the auditorium after the service.

David felt compelled to go forward for prayer, but he was sitting in the balcony and thought it might be more trouble than it was worth to go to the front of the auditorium. But he went anyway. When he got to the front, an older man was waiting to greet him. David didn't remember what he looked like or his name, he just remembered his starched white shirt. When the man asked if he could pray for David, David fell against him, hugging him, and began to cry. The man prayed for him for several minutes, and when David pulled away, much to his embarrassment there was blood all down the front of the older man's starched white shirt. He couldn't remember doing it, but he must have hit his nose.

David began to apologize profusely, but the older man stopped him. He didn't say anything profound or flowery. He simply said, "It was my privilege to pray for you."

David tried to explain the impact of this experience: "I don't know what happened, but I just got it. Right then, I believed that Jesus bled and died for me, because He loved me. I can't explain it," David continued, "but I *feel* forgiven."

David's seemingly small choices—to continue attending church, to read the Scriptures, to go forward for prayer, to seek One whom he could not see—resulted in this experience of being forgiven. Time that we often think is wasted, because we can't measure any results, is well spent, because it is in this process that God "calls those things which do not exist as though they did."[9] It was not David's self-help that brought him this spiritual experience. It was his weak devotion, his fainthearted, prone-to-discouragement soul that remained open to something or Someone other than himself.

If you feel stuck in your recovery from addiction, mired down in an exhausting determination to be "good," feeling deflated and distant from God, I want to encourage you to stay on your tiptoes, looking with a steady gaze for the One who is Other. How we need Him—One who is eternal when we feel bogged down in time, One who is love when we are filled with self-contempt, One who is powerful when we feel impotent, One who is forgiveness when we feel unforgivable.

I have a friend who struggles with same-sex attraction who often feels the pull into an addictive lifestyle of one casual and risky relationship after another. While he sorts out his sexuality, he has made a decision to be abstinent in sexual relationships. Recently he told me about a night when the temptation of a few hours of oblivion from his confusion, loneliness, and disappointment seemed too much to bear. He dropped into a nightclub where he had met men before. As soon as he walked in, he felt like easy prey for all-too-eager participants in meaningless, disconnected sex. He had discovered that just as in the heterosexual world, in the gay lifestyle, there are many who act as if sex is just biology deep. My friend knows, though, that our private parts are connected to our hearts, and when we engage in "casual sex," we fuse our hearts to another's. He had experienced the pain that came from joining another, only to rip off a part of his heart when that relationship ended. He didn't want to do that anymore.

But at the club that night, the opportunities for a quick "fix" literally surrounded him. The minute he walked in the door, he spotted one man who seemed to follow him. After the harrowing experience of physically pulling himself away from the attentions of several men, he decided to leave the club. Near the exit he saw that the same man was still following him. As he left, he turned around and asked the stranger in exasperation, "What is your name?" My friend was impacted physically, emotionally, and spiritually when his follower answered, "Jesús."

Of course the man was merely telling his name, a common name among the large Hispanic population in the Denver area, but my friend wondered if this stalker represented Someone else with a similar name. I don't know whether God used the stranger in the nightclub to remind my friend of what he really wanted, or whether it was just a serendipitous occurrence, but I do believe that every small choice of our wills to be open to Love has eternal relevance. Every movement of our hearts toward God matters. We may not feel something immediately (that's what addicts want), but God continues to open doors into greater love.

Wherever you stand today in the journey of redemption, know that there is a doorway open to greater intimacy. Are you willing to be open to knowing the depths of God's heart for you? That is an intimacy that will not be exhausted, may never be fully comprehended, and cannot be controlled, but it is the intimacy that we were ultimately made for. In the next chapter we will take a longer look at God's heart.

I think about David, courageously and persistently remaining open to God as he walked down to the front of that auditorium, lifting up his weak faith to something unseen. "I imagine Jesus, with eyes as flames of fire, turning to His Father and exclaiming, *'Look at [him], Father! He has not seen Me yet [he] believes! [He] is once more lifting [his] eyes to Me. [He] has chosen to fix [his] gaze again upon what is unseen. How [he] conquers My heart with [his] lovesick gaze!'* "[10]

HARD WORK IN THE MIDST OF HOPELESSNESS

Whether you believe in Jesus and want what David experienced, or not, it is part of the human condition to long for this mystery that merges daily life with a grace that transports us beyond ourselves. In fact, that is part of the energy of addiction. We seek the mysterious, the ecstatic. Every addiction initially seduces the addict into believing that ecstasy can be prolonged. Ecstasy, from *ex stasis,* means "to stand out from," to be free from the tension of the division between subject and object that pervades human experience.

A simple example of the conflict between ecstasy and the mundane came years ago, when our family took a drive into the mountains to see the changing leaves. The shimmering golden aspen leaves seemed to dance against the regal evergreens. My daughter viewed the scenery through the lens of adolescent drama. She wanted to take pictures of every scene along the way, and at each turn in the road, she pronounced the new scenery to be "the most beautiful that she had ever seen in her whole entire life!" And then she sighed, "I could just melt into the trees." She experienced a moment of ecstasy—and then the inevitable disappointment in heading down the mountain. I remember how her disgruntled mood infected the whole family. I fought off an intruding thought that follows many moments of sheer pleasure: *It would have been better not to have gone at all.*

For the addict, we have found a central activity that seduces us with the promise that whatever is wrong in us can be fixed by something outside of us, and we can control it—we can keep it going. This is so close to what we were made for that it can be confusing. We were made for something Other, something or Someone to take us out of ourselves. We get into trouble when we think we are in control of this Other—by being good or doing all the right steps or following certain rules. This last addiction plunges us into vicissitudes of hope and despair, because it is all dependent upon us. Instead of using drugs, alcohol, or sex to overcome the pain of life, to overcome despair, we chase euphoria through self-effort.

The hard work of transformation is founded upon a humility that embraces my own inability to make my life work. When I free up the energy I've used to flee from the imperfect realities of life, I can rest in an openness that is redemptive. The addict can then experience moments of ecstasy and days of despair without having to create her own escape. She is surprised by grace and not surprised by failure while she trusts in a for-giveness that is greater than herself. She is committing to going to whatever lengths necessary to change her addictive behaviors, accepting that it is a mystery why she sometimes *feels* free and other times she doesn't.

David has been walking this path of transformation for *five years,* and he would tell you that he still has a lot of work to do. He still needs individual and marriage therapy. He needs to be in a group with other men, and to be proactive in his life of faith by attending church, reading his Bible, and spending time in quiet meditation. I remember that when David first began therapy and I suggested that this process might be a long one, he balked. Like most addicts, he wanted a quick fix. So I know that redemption is at work in his life right now, because he doesn't have to be in control of the process, he doesn't need all of the answers, and if anyone asks him about his progress, he simply responds, "I've really just begun."

> If you want to find meaning, stop chasing so many things.
>
> —JAPANESE PROVERB

Anita's Story: Nourished by Cotton Candy

> The great preoccupation with things like food and shopping
> and appearance, in turn, is less of a genuine focus on
> hunger—indulging it, understanding it, making decisions
> about it—than it is a monumental distraction from hunger.
> —Caroline Knapp, *Appetites*[1]

Anita wanted everyone to like her. She worked very hard to avoid conflict. She planned what she would say to get the desired response. She collected relationships as proof that she was worthwhile. And she lived with a sense of profound loneliness. People pleasing, seeking affirmation, is about as nourishing as cotton candy but as addicting as cocaine. This addiction is a hard one to acknowledge and change: it looks good, and there is no support group for people who are too nice. But it erodes the soul and swallows up the self just as surely as any addiction. Anita wanted help for her loneliness, seeking what she was surely made for—relationships—but relapsed many times because she often avoided the lifeblood of true relationships—intimacy.

Intimacy has been defined as living with a posture that says "into me see." A person standing this way doesn't crouch in hiding and doesn't tower over others in arrogance. When I interact in this posture, I am willing to be vulnerable, because I want to be known and to know others. I want to be known so that I can receive love, not gain approval. I want to know others so that I can give love, not impress or control. In this chapter we will look at intimacy and the way it can turn loneliness from a force that propels us into relational addictions to the ground that grows the most sustaining nourishment.

This was not Anita's first identified addiction. As a teenager and later in her midthirties, she struggled with eating disorders. In adolescence she had bouts of anorexia, and in midlife she struggled with what she described as the "binge-and-purge hell of bulimia." The recurrence of her eating disorder had brought her into counseling.

Aimee Liu, a former model and anorexic, gives clues in her new book *Gaining: The Truth About Life After Eating Disorders* as to why Anita might have become particularly vulnerable to an eating addiction again:

> [In] adolescence and midlife your looks are changing—and our culture tends to look at women at these ages and judge them so incredibly on how they look. So at both points, if you don't have a really secure sense of self, you become vulnerable.... Women in midlife tend to fall into an eating disorder when there's a loss—a parent dies, a career or child is lost...anything like that can trigger it. But again, it's a combination of unbearable loss, the culture devaluing them because of how they look, and genetic predisposition.[2]

When I first began working with Anita, I understood to some extent how the compulsion and obsession about eating and body image held her captive, but I was not yet aware of her addiction to people pleasing and its added torture. Anita is one of many women that I have worked with who are still struggling with an eating disorder in midlife or later. I have known many women who find some freedom from the behaviors of an eating disorder only to continue to struggle with depression and other addictions. I have discovered that the "wiring" of these women sets them up for a lifetime of compulsive behavior. Often their genetics contribute to an addictive vulnerability, but they also share distortions in thinking.

Women who struggle with eating disorders and relational addictions often have confused desire or passion with compulsion. Passion leads a person to participate in activities or experiences that build faith, like church, a small group, a book club, or a support group. Passion leans into the future by fueling interest in hobbies, creativity, or learning about new subjects. And passion is the lifeblood of relationships. It keeps us inviting, attending, remembering, and creating times with others. I began with Anita, as I do with many of my clients struggling with addiction, by asking her what she was passionate about. I explained that passion is desire or longing driven by faith, hope, and love. Anita looked at the floor for several minutes before she answered, "I can't think of anything right now." She felt ashamed. The people-pleaser part of her knew that she should come up with an answer, but the addicted part of her was tired and drained from thinking about her fat thighs, whether she should try the Jenny Craig diet or just buy some TrimSpa at Walgreens, how many calories were in a grilled chicken sandwich, and whether or not she would take extra laxatives that night.

Anita sighed, "I can't believe I'm in this place again. I thought I'd conquered my eating stuff when I was in college. How did this happen to me?"

Compulsion actually kills passion. It is driven by fear:

- I can't be fat, or I won't be lovable.
- I can't have people mad at me, or they might not like me.
- I can't express my own opinion, because that might make someone mad.
- I have to exercise, or else I will be fat.

- I can't eat certain foods, because they will make me gain weight.
- I can't express certain emotions, because that will cause people to reject me.
- I don't want to make people uncomfortable, or they won't want to be around me.
- I have to purge myself of anything I eat, or I will gain weight.
- I can't be angry, because that will make others uncomfortable.
- I can't gain even one pound, because that will result in a larger weight gain.

Understanding in the Midst of Craziness

Experts in the field of addiction often say that genetics "loads the gun" of an addiction and environment "pulls the trigger." I asked Anita to tell me a bit about her family history. As she started naming the members of her family tree, we began to see a pattern of addiction, depression, and anxiety. Understanding biology and family history is important because it makes sense of addiction.

I said to Anita, "Wow. You didn't have a chance. Your biology set you up." Scientists will be debating for years to come which comes first, but the causes are clearly linked: Does biology change the brain and make you vulnerable to addiction? Or does addiction change the brain, setting you up for further addiction?

The Smoking Gun

I asked Anita to tell me about experiences in her growing-up years that might have influenced her relationship with food and body image. She recalled being fourteen years old, in the midst of the hormonal tumult that comes with adolescence. She realized that her body was changing and growing, which was distressing not only to Anita but also to her mother.

Anita repeated for me the messages from her mother that still play in her head today: *"Always take the smallest portion, always eat something before you go out with others so you don't eat too much in front of them, don't eat that or it will go straight to your hips..."*

When Anita was fifteen, her mother handed her a pack of cigarettes and said, "Smoke these. They will take away your appetite and help you lose that extra weight." Anita took her mother's advice. She found power and satisfaction in controlling her appetite and pleasing her mother. Three addictions (smoking, weight control, and people pleasing) were loaded into the gun, with a soul-deadening impact on Anita's life. Taking a look at her biology and history was necessary for Anita to understand her current struggle.

Women often describe a personal relationship with their addiction—it is their friend, their secret love, their personal support. Such addictions often grow in the void of healthy personal relationships and can be set off by a person's response to something that has special meaning for her. Anita's compulsion and obsession with eating, body image, and people pleasing brought her a sense of power and reassured her that she could be okay in the world. Addiction begins as a constant and sometimes inexpensive friend who will bring comfort and control, but it becomes the most compulsive, demanding, and overwhelming relationship in life.

> Alcohol had become too important. By the end it was the single most important relationship in life. Yes: this is a love story. It's about passion, sensual pleasure, deep pulls, lust, fears, yearning hungers. It's about needs so strong they're crippling. It's about saying good-bye to something you can't fathom living without.
>
> —CAROLINE KNAPP, *Drinking: A Love Story*[3]

I knew that for Anita, and for many who struggle with addiction, her central activities were the means of relieving the self from being alone with the self. When she ate to an extreme, she had momentary relief from her own inner, emotional life. When she made others happy or comfortable, she had something that took the place of being alone with herself for at least a brief period of time. When you are not connected to yourself, it is impossible to be connected to others.

I asked Anita about her marriage. She admitted that she kept her husband at arm's length and that he was growing increasingly dissatisfied with her. Her loss of control in her marriage refueled her eating addiction, where she could temporarily gain some sense of control again. Anita explained further, "I keep everything inside. I don't want to burden others with my emotions. I hate anger, conflict, and sadness. I know that my husband is drifting away from me, but I feel hopeless to do anything about it."

Do you see the sabotage of her desire for relationships? Addiction kills the desire for intimacy. It gives the addict an excuse to not be intimate. When being nice and people pleasing stopped working and her husband expressed dissatisfaction, Anita quickly found another familiar focus that would keep her from working on a healthy relationship. Anita was living in a momentum designed to break and control the sorrow of living in a world where intimacy is uncontrollable and unpredictable. She was choosing behaviors that would make sure that she had no intimacy at all.

As Anita began to understand and acknowledge the roots and realities of her addictions, she became more depressed. Anita saw herself as devout and believed that God (like everyone else) judged her according to how nice and pleasing she was. She felt intense guilt about her eating struggles. She felt like a complete failure, doomed to a life of misery.

The Gift of Powerlessness

During one session, I told her a story about my son. He had been praying for God to help him win a karate tournament. When my son did not even place in the competition, he said to me, "I guess God is too busy for stuff like karate."

I asked my client, "What do *you* think?"

She seemed to almost lose her breath. "Think about what?" she asked.

"About God answering prayer. What does He really think of us?"

She didn't answer for a long time. Then she said, "I know what I've always thought. But right now, I'm not sure. I'm trying to believe in God as I've known Him, but I'm having a hard time believing in a God who really hears me, and loves me, and will heal me." She was describing one component of her overwhelming sense of powerlessness. Anita was expressing more than just an inability to believe: this was a fear that she didn't make an impact on God—a sense of powerlessness at the core of her being. This feeling of powerlessness is more sustained than a crisis of faith, but it can be a gift. When we believe that we earn God's love and merit His help in our lives, we get trapped in the last addiction. Real life teaches us that being good does not always equal having the good life; bad things do happen to good people. Does that mean that God isn't moved by our efforts? Are we powerless to get Him to love us? Yes. And thank goodness. If we believe that we have to be really good, that's perpetually exhausting. If we believe that God is good and can be trusted to love us regardless of how good we are, that's good news. But it is also completely out of our control, and that's unsettling. I was hoping that Anita's sense of powerlessness would lead her to understand that she didn't want to impact God, she wanted to control Him.

Powerlessness fuels addiction but can also be a source of its redemption. We feel powerless in aspects of our lives other than just our relationship with God. Powerlessness makes us believe that what we do doesn't make a difference. All efforts to alter one's world are ineffective. You can't make your parents get back together, you can't make your husband really hear you, you can't make your wife understand how hard you work, and you can't make your children act respectful. When powerlessness is not seen as a gift, we respond by trying to kill the suffering self, which makes us vulnerable to addiction.

Addiction is a sometimes slow but always certain killing of hope. If you want nothing in or from relationships, then you have no sense of despair when you are disappointed. The sign of a person who has lost his hope and his very self to addiction is that he will not live by his own convictions, choices, passions, and feelings. The experience of addiction is that *I will focus on my central activity, and then it won't matter if I can't make an impact on my world. At least no one will get to me.* When people believe that they are powerless to alter their worlds, they will be at risk for an addiction. The paradox is that the addiction ensures their ineffectiveness.

Powerlessness, this sense of being unable to control others or God, can become a gift when it shifts the focus from the world around us—the exterior reality—to the inner world. We often are truly powerless to change the people and circumstances that surround us.

I asked Anita, "Do you think you have what it takes to deal with the external world?"

Her answer revealed her second, more subtle addiction. She responded, "I think I am good at making people feel happy. I usually know what to do and say to put people at ease." Most of us who are people pleasers have very similar stories. Usually early in life, we experienced a parent who rejected us or withheld love, waiting for us to perform well before he or she would love us. We began to believe that if we said or did the right thing, we could win our parent's love and feel okay in the world. Sadly, contorting ourselves to please others actually separates us from ourselves. This addiction is as serious and debilitating as any of the others we have discussed. People pleasing results in losing yourself to others. You know how they feel and what they need, but you don't have a clue as to what you feel and what you need.

One of my favorite professors in graduate school often reminded us, "It is the flight from sorrow that leads to a loss of all hope."[4] I asked Anita to begin a feelings journal, to write about times when she felt sad, afraid, angry, glad, or guilty. I wanted Anita to begin to feel the agonizing emptiness and ache against which she defended herself with her addictions. During those weeks of journaling, she told me that she often felt as if she was in the middle of a hurricane, afraid that she might drown. When you have spent a lifetime not feeling, it is hard to believe that feeling is a necessary part of the process of redemption. I quoted a few fragments from a favorite poem of mine by Wendell Berry:

I let go of all holds then, and sank
like a hopeless swimmer into the earth.[5]

The gift of powerlessness is that it can compel us to let go. This is expressed most succinctly in the first step of Alcoholics Anonymous: "We admitted that we were powerless over [our addiction] and that our lives had become unmanageable." As Anita let go of trying to defend herself against pain, disappointment, anger, and hurt, she found that she was paradoxically experiencing

> We need to recall that God's will never enters where self-will dominates. That's all the admission of powerlessness is. It is a shutting-off of self-will in a particular area.
>
> —JOE McQ, *The Steps We Took*[6]

more joy and hope. She admitted that she was withdrawn and manipulative in her marriage, and she told her husband that she wanted to begin again with their relationship.

Unfortunately, when things got tough in their work on their marriage, Anita's eating disorder would intensify. It was extremely difficult for her to open up and experience intensity, conflict, pleasure, or connectedness. When she felt exposed, she retreated to the covering provided by her eating addiction. Often when we begin identifying feelings, we don't go on to the next important part of this work—identifying what we need. When Anita felt loneliness, depression, or anger, she could not tell what she needed, so she went into her default mode, believing she needed to binge and then purge.

During one session Anita acknowledged that she felt completely alone in her struggles. I asked her, "What do you think you need?" She began by reciting all the things she thought she should be doing, a familiar pattern for people pleasers.

"No," I countered, "what do you need?" Tears formed at the corners of Anita's eyes. "I think I need friends, people who know me and accept me," she answered. I knew that after a person identifies a need, the next question is extremely important: "Is that a realistic expectation?" As Anita and I talked about this need, Anita acknowledged that in order to develop authentic friendships, she would have to be honest and vulnerable, that it was unreasonable to expect real friendships to develop otherwise. I urged Anita to find a support group, but she was afraid that would be too much exposure for her. She knew from her past experience with an eating disorder that it was important to nurture herself with good food, but she still didn't believe that it was important to nurture herself with good relationships.

COMMUNITY IN THE MIDST OF ISOLATION

"I'm so disgusted with myself," Anita began at one of our counseling sessions. "Last night," she continued, as I sensed shame creep onto the couch next to her, "I ate a whole box of macaroni and cheese and then I tried to throw up, but I couldn't even make myself vomit. What is wrong with me? Why do I keep doing this?"

I took a risk and mimicked Anita's words in a similar contemptuous voice, "Anita, what *is* wrong with you? And why do you keep doing the same stupid things over and over again?"

Anita looked at me, shocked. She didn't know what to say.

"Who do I sound like?" I asked.

"I guess you sound like me, but that's how I feel," she answered.

"I suspect you learned that harsh tone from someone else," I explained. "And as long as you respond to yourself with such contempt, you will continue to feel neglected and unloved. When you don't get the nourish-

> If you are going it alone with God, you are probably going it alone.
>
> —STERLING THOMAS, *Sacred Hearts*[7]

ment that you need from your own inner voice, you'll keep reaching for the macaroni and cheese."

As Anita thought about it, she acknowledged that whenever she started to feel lonely, tired, angry, or even physically hungry, she heard her mother's harsh voice:

"*You'd have more friends if you were friendlier.*"

"*You wouldn't be so tired if you went to bed earlier.*"

"*You don't really feel that way.*"

"*If you keep eating like that, you're going to be a fatty.*"

I asked Anita to practice "going inside" herself in response to her feelings and speaking to herself with a nurturing voice. I suggested that she use the voice she might use to speak to her dog or a grandchild. Anita dutifully followed my suggestions. After all, her people-pleaser personality compelled her to be a "good" client! After several weeks of practice she admitted to me, "I'm trying to talk to myself, but I still feel like I'm not really there. I'm still numb."

Anita was the equivalent of an emotional anorexic. She simply would not allow anything in—even from herself—that might nourish her. "I just can't do it," Anita sighed in exasperation.

"Will you try a group?" I asked again.

"Okay," Anita murmured, without a lot of hope.

Freaks and Misfits

At that time I was facilitating a support group for women struggling with different addictions. Each week I asked one woman to bring a song, a film clip, or something else that reflected what she was thinking about or experiencing in her relationship with addiction. I watched Anita listen carefully and quietly to each of these brave women until it was her turn to bring something in.

The next week she came in with a book of photography by Diane Arbus. I recognized the book as one of my favorites, a collection of photographs of "freaks and misfits" of society. Anita showed the group a picture of a misshapen woman dressed in finery. "That's me," she explained. "I have worked so hard to cover me up. My people pleasing is a costume to cover the ugliness that is me."

I winced at Anita's deeply embedded struggle with self-contempt. "Would you like feedback from the group?" I asked.

The people pleaser in Anita rose to the occasion. "I'd love it," she said.

One by one the members of the group asked Anita questions, affirmed her, and invited her to connection. One woman asked, "What makes you feel so ugly?" Immediately another woman in the group said, "Your eyes are always so kind when others talk. I can't believe how unkindly you feel toward yourself." I watched Anita smile politely as she deflected their comments one by one.

"Are you letting anyone in?" I asked.

"Not really," Anita answered honestly. "I'm so sorry," she said. "But I really can't accept what you're saying."

"Is that because you don't trust the group or you don't trust yourself?" I asked Anita.

"I guess it's both," Anita answered. "You don't really know me," she addressed the group, "so how can you say nice things about me? And if I believe the good things that you're saying, then I might not keep working on my life."

Like many who struggle with addiction, Anita believed that she needed to be hard on herself in order to make any changes. She was convinced that if people really knew her, they would be similarly disgusted with her, so she could not rest in any compassion or kindness. As she looked at the other women in the group, she experienced one of the gifts of community. "I feel so lonely," Anita admitted. Community, as imperfect as it is, can awaken within us the longing for relationship.

"How long have you felt this way?" asked one dear woman, a middle-aged soccer mom addicted to marijuana. She, too, knew the pain of isolation.

"All of my life, I think," Anita answered. She was beginning to tell her story in community, and as she dared to look at the longing in every other woman's face, Anita knew that she didn't have to be alone. Margaret Bullitt-Jonas beautifully wrote of her own healing experience within community: "What saved me? Putting down the food. Finding a story. Speaking the story. Feeling the anger and the pain.... Finding people to listen, people who wouldn't let me settle for overeating but who wanted to hear from me, wanted to know the story. My story."[8]

FORGIVENESS IN THE MIDST OF SHAME

Anita participated in every group session, but she stayed stuck, stuck in her inability to receive. She often expressed her frustration at "not getting it," while she kept retreating to overeating and going through the motions of doing the "right" thing. After the group ended, Anita stopped coming to counseling. I ran into her a few months ago at the grocery store.

"How are you?" I asked.

I saw the veil of self-contempt come down quickly over Anita's face. "Oh, I'm about the same. Still doing the same stupid things. I guess I'm one of your failure stories?" Her last statement was a mixture of shame and curiosity.

I really didn't know what to say. Self-contempt is a powerful force that enables a person to feel in control. If I said, "Oh, you're not a failure," Anita wouldn't believe me and would write me off as disingenuous. If I said, "Yes, you are a big failure," Anita would retreat in anger and hurt. Both pathways were ways to escape connection.

I simply said, "I really miss seeing you," and continued on into the grocery store.

What kept Anita stuck? What keeps those who struggle with addiction in a prison of negativity, self-hatred, and alienation from others? It is the last addiction, a belief that I must somehow be good enough and an honest realization that no matter how hard I try, I can't do it. When these two beliefs stand alone—I must do it and I can't do it—the natural human response is self-contempt.

It is not easy to surrender control, especially of our efforts to be good, feel forgiven, act serenely. The prospect can be terrifying to someone who has believed that being in control is the goal. But being good, feeling forgiven, and experiencing serenity cannot be willed. In fact, the harder we try, the more impossible it all becomes.

The sense of being forgiven—forgiven for my failures, my foolish attempts, my lifelong strategies of being in control—does not result from my effort. That's the last addiction. It comes only from openness.

HARD WORK IN THE MIDST OF HOPELESSNESS

Openness is most profoundly revealed in prayer. Prayer that comes out of my inability to "do it" finally leaves room for God. It acknowledges that I am not god. Thérèse of Lisieux said it best, "Prayer arises, if at all, from incompetence, otherwise there is no need for it."[9]

The main shift that takes place when we live in this posture— *"God, help me. I can't do it. I need You"*—is that we begin experiencing a new self. We stop blaming others or shutting them out. We accept responsibility for who we are and acknowledge our core need of something Other. We stop seeing our lives only in terms of who has hurt us and who can't be trusted, and begin to see who we have hurt and our need for forgiveness.

Anita still continued to see herself as victim, victim of others and of her own choices. Her injuries from others and from herself became barriers to relationship rather than the means to a healing relationship that would give her courage to be vulnerable in relationships again. Anita had reached the point of acknowledging the truth about her life, but she would not surrender to the Truth that would set her free. She continued to be her own god, believing that the answer to her struggles was her own effort, but she plunged into greater despair when she failed to achieve her goals.

Perhaps you identify with Anita. You've tried everything and continue to find yourself in the bondage of an addiction. The experience of trying so hard, only to find yourself picking up the pieces once again, is debilitating and confusing. Or maybe you have a family member who struggles with addiction. You find this chapter is discouraging, even a little scary. You're afraid I'm saying that your loved one should stop trying and simply start praying.

I'm not. The hard work of experiencing redemption in the midst of addiction requires that I take complete responsibility for the harm I have inflicted on myself and others due to my addictions. When I fully and deeply acknowledge my responsibility in all of this, I know—heart and soul—that I need a forgiveness that I cannot grant to myself. A profound transformation begins when I know—heart and soul—that I have been completely forgiven. I am able to rejoin human community without shame and contempt when I know that I have been forgiven.

After my relapse I went through the twelve steps of Alcoholics Anonymous with a sponsor. When I came to the ninth step—"Made direct amends to such people wherever possible, except when to do so would injure them or others"—I was terrified. I couldn't imagine asking forgiveness from my children, my parents—my ex-husband. Wouldn't that just open the door to more shame and condemnation? And besides, they had hurt me and misunderstood me. Why open the door to more hurt?

One night I was on the mental merry-go-round of these realities. I wanted to be free of the guilt and shame, but I was too afraid to seek forgiveness, and I really couldn't *feel* God's forgiveness. I believed that Jesus died on the cross for my sins, but I also honestly believed that there were some sins that I would have to pay for for the rest of my life.

I picked up my Bible and turned to an often-quoted verse of Scripture: "In kindness he takes us firmly by the hand and leads us into a radical life-change."[10] In kindness. Could I believe in the kindness of God? Or to use another principle from the twelve steps, could I turn my life over to the *care* of God? (Third step: "Made a decision to turn our will and our lives over to the care of God…") I recalled Brennan Manning's words:

> The tenderness of Jesus frees us from embarrassment about our-
> selves. He lets us know that we can risk being known, that our emo-
> tions, sexuality, and fantasies are purified and made whole by his
> healing touch, and that we don't have to fear our fears about our-
> selves. The wisdom gleaned from tenderness is that, as ragamuffins

entrusted by God, we can trust ourselves and thereby learn to trust others. When the healing tenderness lays hold of our hearts, the false self, ever vigilant in protecting itself against pain and seeking only approval and admiration, dissolves in the tender presence of mystery.[11]

I remembered a time years ago, when my daughter was learning to swim. She loved to stand on the side of the pool and jump into my arms. She could paddle to the side of the pool and jump again and again, for what seemed like hours. I was always careful to make sure that her life preserver was fastened securely around her little body before we began our game of jump, catch, and release. One afternoon we had played until we were both exhausted. I took her to the side of the pool, unfastened her life preserver, and dried her off. I told her that she needed to rest for a while. I headed to the deep end of the pool to dive and swim by myself.

After one dive I came

> I guess we're simply not meant to understand some things. Bono, of U2, who is a Christian, says that his favorite song is "Amazing Grace" and his second favorite is "Help Me Make It Through the Night," and most of the time, I have to let it go at that.
>
> —ANNE LAMOTT, *Plan B*[12]

to the surface and saw my three-year-old toddler running toward the deep end. I was barely catching my breath when Kristin leaped into the middle of the pool toward me. My hands reached blindly toward her as she plunged beneath the water. Somehow I was able to tread water and grab her.

"Honey, what are you doing?" I exclaimed.

With a look of pure joy, she said, "Mommy, I knew you would catch me!"

I have never forgotten the feeling of my heart being stuck in my throat as I held back a harsh admonition. I couldn't bear to discipline her because of her fierce trust in me.

That night as I pondered my recovery from addiction, I wondered if I could just jump like that into the kindness of God and trust Him with the results. I prayed a prayer that I have prayed a thousand times since then: "God, forgive me. Help me believe."

Two nights after these ponderings, I announced to my then fourteen-year-old daughter that I was going to the grocery store.

"Are you sure that's where you're going?" she asked suspiciously.

I saw the evidence of my relapse on her face. She lived with a fear that it could happen again. One of the great costs of my alcoholism was that I had betrayed my daughter's trust. She wasn't so ready to jump anymore.

> Leap, and the net will appear.
>
> —JULIA CAMERON, *The Artist's Way*[13]

"Oh, honey," I said. "I am so sorry that you're afraid. I'm sorry that I hurt you by drinking. Will you please forgive me?"

Kristin jumped in. "Mom, I already forgave you. I'm just glad that you're not drinking."

My daughter's response reminded me that forgiveness cannot be demanded of others or of myself. It surprises us in the midst of our willingness.

8

JIM'S STORY: SEX, DRUGS, AND ROCK'N'ROLL

> You do not have to change for God to love you.
> Be grateful for your sins. They are carriers of grace.
> —ANTHONY DE MELLO, *Wellsprings*[1]

J im is my brother. His is a story of years of struggle with alcohol, cocaine, and meth. During the nineties, Jim was the lead singer of an industrial metal band called Rorschach Test. It took him more than a few years to read the signs in his own life and understand what all his crazy addictive behavior was about. Jim did his detox in a jail cell. In the process, he discovered that his drug addiction was a sort of spiritual reversal. I've learned a lot from Jim about drug addiction, but he has taught me even more about seeking a spiritual life from the inside out rather than the other way around.

Jim did not set out to be a bona fide, chart-topping heavy metal rock star. No, instead he began his adult life as a bright, talented, ordained minister. He could easily translate the Greek and Hebrew of Scripture and was especially gifted in speaking words of faith to his congregation. What moved him from the pulpit to prison? How did his passion shift from the things of God to drugs and alcohol? The answers to these questions can help us understand the momentum of addiction.

Jim's story reveals that even a life steeped in religion does not protect from or solve addiction. After studying many addicts, Dr. William Silkworth comes to this conclusion in the "Big Book" of Alcoholics Anonymous: "[U]nless [a] person can experience an entire psychic change there is very little hope of his recovery."[2] *An entire psychic change.* In fact, it is often the realities of addiction that help save us, that reveal to us—more powerfully than any sermon or intellectual grasp of theology—true spirituality, what it means to *experience* a total psychic change.

Jim tells his story of church and altar calls as well as cocaine and sold-out concerts, not to glamorize his experience in the music industry or to denigrate his experience in the church, but to reveal the truth of the human condition—that there are longings within each of us that pull on us more strongly than any addiction. Jim's fellow musician and addict Kurt Cobain wrote in his journal, "When you wake up this morning, please read my diary. Look through my things, and figure me out."[3] Sadly, Cobain never figured himself out. Addiction took his life when he was only twenty-seven. Whether a person is a pious man or woman in the church or an out-of-control musician in the entertainment world, we all risk trying to soothe the deep cravings of our souls by our own efforts, only to find that we have completely lost ourselves along the way. I am grateful for my brother's courage in looking at himself and finding help to guide him on this journey.

No matter what we accomplish or accumulate, if we are honest, we have to admit that our souls always desire more. Jim's story reveals an earnestness and a recklessness in trying many avenues, from seminary to the world of rock'n'roll, only to find that the emptiness within was even greater than it was before. I asked Jim to write about his experience with addiction. Here is his story, in his own words:

I grew up in a very strong fundamentalist, Bible-believing home. I have extremely vivid memories from a very young age of my Sunday school teacher, my childhood pastor, and even my mother telling me how to be sure that I would escape the eternal fires of hell. I also have many terrifying memories of that time, because in spite of the good-intentioned efforts of the aforementioned evangelists, I simply did not understand. I spent countless long nights of terror-filled agony praying variations of the prayer, "Jesus, please come into my heart," over and over again. This continued throughout my entire childhood and even into the beginning of my adolescence—right up until that magical summer of 1981.

That summer at a church camp I heard a sermon by a preacher from Alabama. He sounded a whole lot like Elvis when he preached. He looked into the audience that hot July night and said, "There is probably someone right here tonight who is wondering if they have done everything absolutely right to be saved. You have said your prayers a million times, but you still are not sure if God has heard you. You have tried so hard and have wondered if you have tried hard enough. Well, you can stop wondering and trying, because the Lord Jesus Christ has already done and completed absolutely every-thing necessary for you to be saved. When He said, "It is finished," He meant it. He finished the work so that He could have a relation-ship with you."

Suddenly it was as if the light came on. I believed. All of the confusion made sense. This was not about whether or not I had done everything, said everything, prayed everything. This was about having a relationship with Someone who had already done everything for me.

I wanted to learn everything that I could about this new

relationship. Suddenly all that did not appeal to me about Christianity became intriguing and exciting.

I wanted to be around the people that I once dreaded and even feared. I wanted to go to the places I once avoided—church, home Bible studies, etc. I wanted to learn all about the religious practices—communion, the doxology, different creeds of faith.

I even learned a new language—Christianspeak. The words rolled off my tongue: "Amen. Praise the Lord! You are such a blessing to me. I'll be praying for you."

I became willing to do anything required of me in order to experience a deeper level of devotion. I was drawn to those who had made a total commitment to faith—to pastors and those in full-time ministry. They often indicated that they thought that maybe it was God's plan for me to be one of them. I was becoming more and more willing to give it all.

I went to Bible college and seminary and became a licensed pastor. I found a position as the assistant to the senior pastor in a small church—the very church that I had grown up in. Suddenly my whole life was set in order right before me. My path and my future were clear.

This was truly the most exciting time in my life. I never experienced anything that packed the thunder of that summer of 1981.

Except maybe the summer of 1990. That was the first time that I tried cocaine. That was just after the church that I had grown to love asked me to leave.

I met a girl on my rise to ordination at one of the summer Bible conferences that I attended who told me that she was also called to a life of deeper devotion to God. We fell in love and married shortly after I graduated from seminary. One Sunday evening I returned home from a weekend youth retreat and found my wife curled in a tight ball upon our bed. When I asked her what was wrong, she finally told me. She had been having an affair for the last six months and didn't love me anymore. In fact, she didn't even think that she believed in God. She wanted a divorce.

I ran to my senior pastor and in tears he hugged me. He said that he was sorry and that he would be praying for me. The following Monday morning I received a telephone call from the lead elder on the church board informing me that I had been relieved of my duties.

I was devastated. Suddenly the life that I thought was set before me completely unraveled. I was hurt and confused. Fear began to set in. What had I done that was so wrong? Where was God in all of this?

A few weeks later I responded to an ad in the newspaper that basically stated, "If you have a pulse we will hire you." I began to work at a collections agency where I met someone who introduced me to cocaine. Right after I snorted my first line, it was like my eyes opened and the light came on. I wanted to learn everything that I could about this new relationship.

Suddenly all that did not appeal to me about drug use became intriguing and exciting.

I wanted to be around the people that I once dreaded and even feared. I wanted to go to the places I once avoided.

I wanted to learn all about the rituals associated with drug use—the hunt, chopping, sealing, cooking, hot-knifing, rolling bills, cutting straws, and using pens.

I even learned a new language—Drugspeak. New words rolled off my tongue—snow blow cola, a fine white teenager, "Do you want guns or roses?"

I became willing to do anything required of me to experience a deeper level of devotion. I was drawn to those who had made a total commitment to drugs—full-time "ministers" or dealers. I was becoming more and more willing to give it all. I did not become one of the "ministers," but I did join the choir.

UNDERSTANDING IN THE MIDST OF CRAZINESS

Jim's saga of sex, drugs, and rock'n'roll ends like that of many others in the entertainment industry. He ran out of money, out of gigs, and out of chances. He ended up in a jail in Washington State. He will tell you that prison was a horrendous way to go through detox—no tranquilizers or soft mattresses to ease the pain. All that his holding cell offered was a single torn page from the Bible. It was a page from the Old Testament, and the words on that page were not particularly meaningful, but he held on to it for dear life. In his trembling hands that held the page of Scripture, in his fuzzy thinking, and even in his debilitating shame, he was reminded of his childhood cravings, longing to know God and hoping that knowing would give him answers about his place in this world.

During the lonely and agonizing days in that jail, Jim acknowledged that for his whole life, he had been trying to satisfy an insatiable part of his very being. His childhood pursuit of an escape from hell, his attendance at seminary, his ministerial position, his drug use to escape the hell on earth that he was experiencing, the formation of his band, and his musical career—all were attempts to feed his soul.

I understood Jim's thirst. I too can look back to summer-camp experiences and years of exceptional performance—never missing a chance to be listed in the National Honor Society or in *Who's Who in American Colleges and Universities*—and to years of saying, "I can't keep doing this anymore. It isn't satisfying." Like my brother, I found a quicker and easier way to experience a few moments of escape and relief from the deeper cravings of my soul. Through it all, I've always sensed a longing, a longing that often felt like emptiness, and an emptiness that I interpreted as thirst. What I didn't know was that my thirst was for Love. Instead I discovered liquor, and I began to crave the power of alcohol. The way it burns. The way it burns away fear and disappointment. Liquor seemed better than love. It was very reliable, and it wouldn't leave me. But like Jim, I was still thirsty.

Soul Thirst

This craving that Jim and I both experienced is rooted in our inner human nature. Psychology has been called "the study of the soul." The root word *psyche* is the Greek word meaning "soul" or "breath." Psychology studies human experience apart from the physical, tangible, visible world. If bread and water feed the body, what feeds the soul? What feeds the part of us that yearns for faith and that longs for hope?

Quite simply, it is love. We are designed to be driven by love, driven *to* love. Perhaps the purest form of love that we experience comes when we are babies, when we are loved for simply being. Jesus said, "Unless you accept God's kingdom in the simplicity of a child, you'll never get it."[4] The soul never stops thirsting for more of that experience. Sadly, however, painful human experiences drive us away from love. We learn that love comes with strings attached, that love is dependent upon our performance, that love can disappear without warning.

When Jim began his spiritual journey, the messages he received were not about love and acceptance, but about fear and condemnation. He moved from the simplicity of a child to the complexity of the adult world, believing that spirituality comes from what you do on the outside. Jim was taught that our résumés prove our spirituality and guarantee our place in the kingdom. In other words, Jim's deep need for love became a legalistic matter.

When Jim heard the southern preacher proclaiming the good news of

Love—that you can't save yourself and it's not up to you—something awakened within his spirit. He found fellowship with God's Spirit that came from the inside. But it's hard to rest and stay rooted in a spirituality that is not based on our efforts. We are vulnerable; when life falls through the cracks, we are back to the dilemma of the last addiction: It is up to me, and I can't do it.

When we are seduced by the last addiction, to the treadmill of performance and accomplishment, our souls become parched. When we are hurt or betrayed, the pain of our souls' thirst feels unbearable. We are drawn to anything that might quench our thirst, even for a while. We clamor after people, behaviors, or substances that promise to meet our spiritual need for love. We crave the control of believing that we can meet that need from the outside in, through drugs, alcohol, food, people pleasing, work, or gambling. These things steal our hearts with promises that seem too good to be true, and eventually we discover that they are.

Jim told me about lying on his thin, smelly mattress in the jail cell where his addictions had taken him. There he returned to the truth that had first promised refreshment for his soul, that a spiritual life was not about his performance, good or bad. When he had no other place to go, the paralysis of his soul began to heal as he dared to believe that God loved him just for being. Jim was in a harsh place, but a transformative one. In a similar experience of helplessness, the Jesuit Pedro Arrupe composed a powerful prayer after he suffered a debilitating stroke. His physical paralysis compelled him to surrender to the only hope for his soul. I return to his prayer as I consider my own addictions and those of others I love. Arrupe knows the gifts that come in addiction: being freed to acknowledge our deep thirst and our inability to satisfy it:

> More than ever I find myself in the hands of God. This is what I
> have wanted all my life from my youth. But now there is a differ-

ence; the initiative is entirely with God. It is indeed a profound spiritual experience to know and feel myself so totally in God's hands.[5]

COMMUNITY IN THE MIDST OF ISOLATION

Many communities of support are available to those recovering from drugs and alcohol, especially in Twelve Step meetings. But finding community is not easy for a recovering fundamentalist. It takes a great deal of humility for a recovering minister and rock star to sit in a church basement with other addicts and acknowledge the painful truths of his life. Perhaps it just takes an insatiable thirst. One of the gifts of addiction is that we addicts know that we have a thirst, a hunger, a desire that cannot be satisfied, no matter how hard we try. This unquenchable thirst can take us back to the liquor store or it can push us to go to an Alcoholics Anonymous meeting, attend a church worship service, call a friend for coffee, read a book of prayers and meditations, or pay a visit to a suffering fellow addict.

Relief for the thirsty soul requires humility. You must be humble to take a sip of refreshment when you know that you will still be a bit thirsty, if not today, then again tomorrow. It takes humility to learn from others how to find Living Water. In humility, we surrender to the reality that God is not interested in quenching our thirst completely. He intends to be investigated for eternity, which means that we will always remain thirsty for something—for Him. Humility accepts that there is an insatiable longing. In the psalmist's words, we're "the hart pant[ing] after the water brooks."[6]

During the past month I have watched the beginning episodes of this season's *American Idol* and thought a lot about the difference between humility and humiliation. What is our fascination with watching untalented people make complete fools of themselves, only to be humiliated by Simon and the other judges? Don't the contestants know that they can't sing, that in fact, they are awful at it? Maybe that is why we watch. The competitors may be taking our place. We harbor fears that there is something deeply wrong with us, that we'll reveal our flaws and experience the shame of being fools. This whole phenomenon explains why we avoid community. We are afraid that we won't be noticed, and then that we will be, and that the end result will be more pain and humiliation. Defending ourselves, we become bitter, skeptical, and cynical, which only intensifies the thirst of our souls for love.

Our thirst for love, and the foolish schemes that we have followed looking for it in all the wrong places, reveal the essential truth *that we belong together.* Last spring I volunteered to deliver Meals on Wheels in our community. I was paired with a woman in her midfifties to deliver to a route of about twenty-five homes. Most of the recipients were elderly, shut in their homes due to physical limitations. My partner was also a recovering alcoholic, and we enjoyed sharing our experiences as we delivered the meals.

One house on our route was home to a young family—a husband, wife, and two small children. The husband was confined to a wheelchair; he had been in a car accident that left him paralyzed from the waist down. One day when I ran in to drop off the warm meal, I found him passed out in his kitchen. His wife hurried into the room, glanced at her husband in his wheelchair, and explained, "Since his accident, he drinks too much. It helps him get through the day."

My heart went out to this suffering man and his family. A few weeks later, my delivery partner and I walked in together with another meal for this household. I had been telling my new friend about my spiritual discoveries in my own journey of recovery when we found our fellow alcoholic passed out again in the kitchen. This time he had fallen from his chair and lay on the floor in a puddle of his own vomit. I called out to his wife, but she didn't come. Repulsed by the sight and smells of this man, I backed out of the kitchen.

"I need some fresh air," I said to my partner.

Standing outside, I watched through the window as my friend knelt beside the man, gently wiped his face, and cleaned up his mess. I decided I would wait a few more weeks before I shared more of my insights with her. She was showing more knowledge of the love of God than I had.

We waited for the man to stir, and then we helped him into his wheelchair. He looked at us, embarrassed, and mumbled, "I just needed something."

Oh, how he needed love. How we all do! It was so plain to me that all of us are crippled and need someone to sit with us, wipe away our tears, and not be disgusted by our messiness. Often we cannot believe in God's love until we have experienced human love. That means we have to take risks in order to find community.

My brother needed to take that risk. A few years into sobriety, he found himself surrounded again by those who believed that spirituality is something that we attain from the outside. It made him mad, mad at the church and mad at God. That is a risk that we take when we seek out others. I don't write this to be discouraging but to be honest. When we have spent a lifetime energized by shame, we are quickly drawn back into experiences that will put us into a familiar place, once again feeling shame. I think this reality lies behind the questions that I am most often asked in my counseling office: "Why do I keep doing the same kind of things over and over again?" or "Why do I end up in relationships with the same kinds of people?" or "Why do I always end up embarrassing myself?"

Shame must be dismantled before we can make different kinds of choices in response to our cravings for love. The only way I know to dismantle shame is to accept, to inhabit, our brokenness. Brokenness acknowledges the truth about my life and speaks the truth in love to others. Brokenness does not fear messiness or demand that the mess be quickly cleaned up. Brokenness embraces forgiveness as the only glue to put the pieces back together. Jim had acknowledged the brokenness of his life, but he still believed that the only way to be accepted was to be better than ever. That is the energy of shame. Sadly, this energy attracted him to a group of people with similar beliefs. Many Christians get trapped in this last addiction, believing that forgiveness is a one-time event and that, after that conversion experience, the rest is up to us. It creates terrible pressure: we need to work to keep ourselves saved.

Forgiveness in the Midst of Shame

Our church supports a group that goes into impoverished third-world countries and provides sources of clean water. I have learned from these engineers that you don't find water simply by tapping into a flowing underground river. Instead, they carefully drill into a place where saturation has occurred, a layer of earth called an aquifer. When they drive a well, they are relieving pressure. Pure water comes then, not under pressure, but when pressure is taken away.

My brother Jim was eventually able to identify the pressure that he was under, pressure that often kept him from receiving Living Water. Like many addicts and people who have grown up in the church, he was resentful toward God. Remember my brother's question in the ruins of his marriage: *Where is God in all of this?* Every person that I have known who struggles with addiction has come face to face with suffering and decided that God can't be trusted. If I can't trust God, then I can't trust other people. If I can't trust God or others, then I have to trust myself. I can't think of anything more terrifying or discouraging than to believe that I am the only one who can be trusted.

This lack of trust also propels us back into hiding, which is the breeding ground of addiction. For Jim, this suspicion about God and others led him to a community that harbored the same distrust. There are many things that make us vulnerable to addiction, but the greatest pitfall is believing that we must hide.

Jim is not stagnant. He is searching and asking a crucial question that I pray will lead to greater brokenness and a further understanding of forgiveness. What do we do with our questions about God? Life is often unfair. Most addicts I know come pretty quickly to a sense that they need to be forgiven, but we are often halted in our spiritual life when we can't consider another type of forgiveness, the need we humans have to forgive God. This might seem like a startling concept to you, but how else can you grapple with tragedy that doesn't make sense? Our thinking brains might be able to acknowledge, in the abstract, that God knows what He's doing, and somehow in the scheme of things, everything will work together for good. But our feeling brains need more. Forgiving God is a way of saying, "I don't understand You, but I trust You. I don't need a neat and tidy explanation of things, but I will be sad about difficult and disturbing realities." This brokenness before God allows us to remain broken with one another.

Regarding those things that we can't understand, I have returned over and over to the experiences of two volunteers who work with terminally ill children. One of them tells a story that poignantly demonstrates what it might mean to have a heart of forgiveness, to recognize the brokenness of human experience, and to respond in creative love.

My idea was pretty simple at the beginning. I started to volunteer in wards with terminally ill children or burn victims—just go in there to cheer them up a little, spread around some giggles. Gradually, it developed that I was going to come in as a clown....

It's a little tricky coming in. Some kids, when they see a clown, they think they're going to be eaten alive. And kids in hospitals and burn units, of course, are pretty shaky....

Burnt skin or bald heads on little kids—what do you do? I guess you just face it. When the kids are really hurting so bad, and so afraid, and probably dying, and everybody's heart is breaking. Face it and see what happens after that, see what to do next.

I got the idea of traveling with popcorn. When a kid is crying, I dab up the tears with the popcorn and pop it into my mouth or into his or hers. We sit around together and eat the tears.[7]

I know that this story is a lot to digest. We can barely get past envisioning the burned and hurting children to even frame questions about where God is in the midst of suffering. If you are feeling overwhelmed by this story, then you can understand what happens in addiction, especially in relapse. We experience shocking, heartbreaking realities and can't think of anything else but "I need to make this go away."

Experiencing brokenness requires that we first of all face it. Feel it. Don't move quickly to make everything okay. Don't come up with trite answers or neat and tidy conclusions. There are some things that we cannot explain and that we should not look at alone. But we do not have to run away. We can engage with the pain.

We sit around together and eat the tears. As my brother and I came together and began to share our sorrows and our struggles and our questions, we stopped trying to come up with answers. We started to forgive God for the shattered circumstances of our lives. Of course, God didn't need our forgiveness. But we needed to forgive Him. In the end, the only thing we can know is who we can trust. Forgiveness is way of saying "I trust you."

By trusting God, we begin to trust community again.

Not too long ago, my brother and I were talking about this again. Quite honestly, he has still not found a large community that he can trust. But he has found a few people, and for now that is enough. Jim is experiencing love and offering it too.

As we talked about addiction and community, truth and trust, I jumped on my soapbox about the suffering that addiction causes. A lot of pain came pouring out of me. In our community in the past six months, we have seen a beautiful young mother and her two children mowed down by a drunk driver, a judge who presides over traffic court pulled over for driving under the influence, and two pastors asked to leave their churches because of secret addicted behavior.

"Somebody needs to do something," I complained to my brother.

"Somebody already has," he answered softly.

HARD WORK IN THE MIDST OF HOPELESSNESS

My brother has not done the work of recovery perfectly. He continues to struggle to find community. Like me, Jim is prone to wandering into the desert of trying to do it all by himself, but he does not waver from remembering who is the Source of spirituality. He quoted to me from the gospel of John, "God is sheer being itself—Spirit. Those who worship him must do it out of their very being, their spirits, their true selves, in adoration."[8]

"Sharon," he said, "Someone paid the price for all this suffering. We can't lose sight of Him."

That is the hard work of staying in the way of redemption, keeping our eyes on Love. How do we stay in the Way when we fail, when we experience inexplicable sorrow, when community falters or sends us back into hiding? We need to remember that our own failures and the failures of others—even in the midst of earnest commitment—reveal our thirst for One who does not fail.

Jesus understands thirst. When He was nailed to the cross, among the last words He uttered were, "I am thirsty."[9] He was suffering in His human body the same brokenness we know ourselves. And He suffered even more, because He let Himself be wrongly crucified, deprived of life by human wrongdoing, accepting the brokenness of humanity in Himself. Jesus chose death because of His love for us. From the tree He whispers, "No more shame. No more hiding. No more justifying. No more working. I condemn sin in the flesh. And you're free, free to love God without fear and shame. *I am thirsty for you to love Me.*"

Jesus's thirst, His love for us and His longing to be loved, is the only reality bigger than our addictions, our sufferings, and our failures in community. In the midst of craziness, understanding will get fuzzy again. Community will fail us, and isolation will seem like a reasonable alternative. Forgiveness will be diminished when shame and suffering resurface, and our perspective will grow dim, threatening to send us back into the quicksand of addiction. Redemptive hard work always returns to Jesus and His view of us from the cross.

When you struggle with an addiction or you have a loved one who does, it is hard, humbling work to remember that the alcoholic is not merely a drunkard, the sex addict is not just a pervert, the drug addict is not someone morally bankrupt seeking another high. No, they are all, *we are all* people thirsty for the One who is thirsty for us.

Pay attention to your soul. It is thirsty for More than a quick fix, a temporary escape, an accumulation of material possessions or accolades, or a neat and tidy life. Love has been looking for you all of His life. I think that's why His story won't go away. On a cross, Jesus died, naked and beaten for love, and His suffering connects to ours when, in the midst of suffering, we look at Him.

I remember a client who decided to take a risk by joining a support group for her eating addiction. She had been closed off, numb, and hidden for so long that she went with great fear and literal trembling. She said to me, "I felt like a lamb going to the slaughter. I felt like a fool." Her words connected her to Jesus, who is described as the lamb of God, slain for the world.[10] She was experiencing pain like His. *What was He thinking, to die for us?* He made a fool of Himself. He gambled everything on the power of love.

I suspect that some of my readers are frustrated once again, wondering, *But what do we do?* Again, I answer, do everything. Find a good therapist to help you understand your story. Join a support group and risk community. Engage in theological discussions with trusted friends about suffering and its meaning in the world. But always, and finally, "Behold the Lamb."

Our intellects and our wills drive us to find a way by ourselves. Even within religion, we create our own paths with systematic theologies and new insights into old truths. Through addiction, we try to find lives apart from suffering and trust. We wander, seeking something central to our lives that we can understand and manage. But our thirsty souls are incorrigible. We can't satisfy them. All this thirst has to be about something besides us. Redemption begins when we don't forget that there is One who is thirsty for us, no matter how good or bad we are. Remembering His thirst doesn't explain everything; it doesn't erase suffering or give us an outline for success. But it does answer our deepest craving—to be loved. When we rest in that love, we can take a breath and return to understanding in the midst of craziness, community in the midst of isolation, and forgiveness in the midst of shame. Believing in Love is *the* hard work, but we can relax right in the midst of it, because Love is even stronger than our unbelief.

Not too long ago, my college-bound son told me he was struggling with faith. "Mom," he said, "I'm not sure that I'm a Christian. In fact, if I hadn't been raised in the church, I don't think I would believe any of this stuff."

My heart started pounding and my palms were sweating as I tried to formulate a brilliant answer that would keep my son on the straight and narrow.

Taking a big gulp, I asked, "What made you start thinking this way?"

"I don't know," he admitted. "I just have a lot of questions and doubts."

Relief flooded over me. "Oh, I understand that," I said. "I do too."

Graham looked at me in surprise.

"The truth is, you can't doubt someone you don't believe in. God can handle your questions," I said.

And then I did what mothers everywhere are guilty of. I took a little trip down memory lane. I reminded Graham of a drive in the car when he was about four years old. In childlike simplicity he had asked me, "Mom, how do you invite Jesus into your heart?"

"Well, you just ask Him," I said.

"Okay," he answered. My little son bowed his head, and I saw his lips silently issuing an invitation.

"Remember that time?" I asked.

"Yeah, Mom," Graham said, "I've met God, and ever since, I haven't been able to get rid of Him."

I smiled. I knew the feeling.

The hard work of seeing redemption in the midst of addiction is summed up by the apostle Paul in the New Testament: "It is [God] who gives to all men life and breath and all things.... He created them to seek God, with the hope that they might grope after Him in the shadows of their ignorance, and find Him."[11]

PART III

THE TRUTH ABOUT REDEMPTION

*Everything in life that we really accept
undergoes a change. So suffering must
become love. That is the mystery.*

—KATHERINE MANSFIELD

Behold, I make all things new.

—REVELATION 21:5, KJV

9

THE PROMISED LAND: LOVING AN ADDICT

> You have no new ideas on how to make it work. You have
> tried everything.... You have been trying so hard to make a
> silk purse out of a sow's ear.... But you can't save yourself,...
> because we are addicted to our allergies, and you are allergic to
> [this relationship]. Stop trying to be your own savior. Give it
> up to God. Let God be your savior. It gets you off the hook,
> and it puts God on the hook, where He belongs.
>
> —ANNE LAMOTT, *Joe Jones*[1]

Well, I certainly hope that the next five years are better than the last five have been," Shirley sighed with a hint of resignation.

"What's been so bad for you these last five years?" I asked.

Shirley and Sid were the parents of one of my closest friends. I'd just met them at a shared Thanksgiving meal.

"What hasn't been bad?" Sid responded irritably.

"Our daughter got a divorce," Shirley began, "and our son is an alcoholic. He has been in two different treatment centers, and last spring he got a DUI. It just seems like it's one thing after another."

There was an uncomfortable pause. Another guest tried to shift the conversation. "Well, it sure sounds rough for your kids. What have you two been up to?"

"What do you mean, 'What have we been up to?' " Sid asked angrily. "We've been doing damage control. We don't have time for a life!"

Shirley saw that we were caught off guard by Sid's angry outburst. "We wouldn't have it any other way, though," she interrupted her husband. "I mean, when your kids suffer, you have to be there for them. They are our life."

Someone at the table complimented the chef on the turkey, and the conversation took another turn. But later that night, I found myself thinking about Sid and Shirley's reflections on their life. I didn't know all of the details, and I certainly did not presume that I could judge them or evaluate their choices, but I recognized something, something I have struggled with myself: the tendency to immerse myself in the lives of people I care about while forgetting to look at myself.

Psychiatrists and psychologists might call this approach to life *co-dependency*. Family counselors might prescribe a course of "tough love." Self-help gurus might encourage Sid and Shirley to take care of themselves, no matter what. However, their situation is more complicated than one-dimensional diagnoses and treatments. Loving an addict immerses you in a world that you would have never chosen. It takes up all the air in the room, leaving you gasping for breath. When you are in a relationship with someone who is struggling with an addiction, you are always scrambling for a solution to the problem and "waiting for the other shoe to drop" at the same time, which leaves very little energy for self-care.

I felt this energy of simultaneous desperation and negligence when I was in Cambodia. We visited the bustling, changing city of Battambang and stayed in the Teo Hotel, right in the commercial district. The door to our room opened to the roof, and we would spend the early mornings and evenings watching the city wake up and close down. Every day, hundreds of merchants set up their tiny stalls amid the teeming crowds of children, goats, and automobiles. Young Cambodians were working desperately to better their lives, to make a profit, become more Western. On almost every corner of the dusty dirt streets, where vendors were selling everything from used cell phones to deep-fried spiders, were plastered large colorful signs that read Tourism—The Way of the Future.

But when the vendors closed their booths and the traffic slowed, we witnessed another side of the city. People shoved mounds of trash along both sides of the streets, right in the middle of the market district. Waves of nauseating stench swept over us from the Stung Sangker River where human waste was dumped. Sent by their parents, young children wandered past the closed-up shops with their hands held out, begging from passersby. This unsettling urban combination of desperation and carelessness struck me as very much like being in a relationship with an addict.

In desperation, believing we are responsible for changing others, we ache, complain, and try to control the addict. We can recite her problems and describe her struggles in great detail—what she thinks, feels, does, and says, as well as what she doesn't think, feel, do, and say. Melody Beattie, author of the best-selling *Codependent No More*, describes the desperation of the man or woman in relationship with an addict:

> We nag; lecture; scream; holler; cry; beg; bribe; coerce; hover over; protect; accuse; chase after; run away from; try to talk into; try to talk out of; attempt to induce guilt in; seduce; entrap; check on; demonstrate how much we've been hurt; hurt people in return so they'll know how it feels; threaten to hurt ourselves; whip power plays on; deliver ultimatums to; do things for; refuse to do things

for; stomp out on; get even with; whine; vent fury on; act helpless; suffer in loud silence; try to please; lie; do sneaky little things; do sneaky big things; clutch at our hearts and threaten to die; grab our heads and threaten to go crazy; beat on our chests and threaten to kill; enlist the aid of supporters; gauge our words carefully; sleep with; refuse to sleep with; have children with; bargain with; drag to counseling; drag out of counseling; talk mean about; talk mean to; insult; condemn; pay for miracles; go to places we don't want to go; stay nearby to supervise; dictate; command; complain; write letters about; write letters to; stay home and wait for; go out and look for; call all over looking for; drive down dark alleys at night hoping to see; chase down dark alleys hoping to catch; run down alleys at night to get away from… placate; provoke; try to make jealous; try to make afraid; remind; inquire; hint; look through pockets; peek in wallets; search dresser drawers; dig through glove boxes; look in toilet tanks; try to look into the future; search through the past; call relatives about; reason with; settle issues once and for all; settle them again; punish; reward; almost give up; try even harder; and a list of other handy maneuvers I've either forgotten or haven't tried yet.[2]

Whew! It's easy to see why there's little energy left for self-care, why we become careless about our own lives.

As you read the list, you might wonder, *Doesn't everyone do some of these things for people they love? Isn't everyone codependent?* Yes, many of these actions are common behaviors in a relationship, but when addiction is part of the relationship, we take these behaviors to another level. We don't "stay on our side of the line." For example, caring what others think can be healthy, but caring so much that I cover up my spouse's bad behavior and make excuses for her is not healthy. Helping others is good, decent behavior, but becoming entangled in a sense of responsibility for making someone else okay, and weighed down with guilt when I can't do it, is not how we were meant to live.

In her wonderful novel *Joe Jones,* Anne Lamott describes the reality of someone who is in an unhealthy relationship with an addict. Louise loves Joe, an alcoholic who drops in and out of her life, depending on his sobriety. Louise is desperate for Joe to stop drinking and negligent of her own hurts and needs in the relationship.

> But it is as if there is a picture of Louise's skeleton, and over it is a transparency showing her muscular system, and over that there's a transparency of her organs, and over that is a transparency of her cardiovascular system, and over that is a transparency of Joe Jones. It is dark gray with regret, depression, anger, and what the poet Lermontov called the bitter record of the heart....
> Yearning, said another poet, is blindness.[3]

Loving an Addict Isn't Easy

I could fill an entire book with the experiences of desperate, careless people I have known who love addicts:

- the husband who looks through his wife's dresser drawers every night, trying to gauge how much she has drunk during the day—while she has been home with their children
- the mother who creeps to the bathroom door while her daughter is inside, to hear whether she is purging—while she herself is steadily gaining weight, eating mindlessly all day long to numb her own pain and worry
- the wife who brings her husband in for counseling for his daily marijuana use—while she is becoming increasingly isolated from family and friends

- the husband who calls every telephone number on his wife's cell phone bill to see whom she is talking to—while he is at risk for losing his job due to poor performance
- the parents who get a second mortgage on their home to pay for their adult son's drug treatment—while they don't talk to each other, go on vacation with each other, or share anything in common except concern for their son

Melody Beattie, in her book *Playing It by Heart,* recounted the relationship of writer Mary Allen with a man addicted to cocaine: "By the time it sunk in that he was an addict, she said it was *too late.* She was seated, strapped in, and along for the ride. She was in love."[4] Beattie described the energy of such a sick love: "At its heart is the struggle to control the uncontrollable, to ensure love and security, to make the unsafe safe."[5] Tragically, as Allen relates in her book *The Rooms of Heaven,* her beloved addict later stuck a gun in his mouth and pulled the trigger.

Are you in a relationship with an addict? You wince at some of my statements in this chapter, and then you get angry, like my friend's father, Sid. You, too, ask bitterly, "What else am I supposed to do?" That is the last addiction taunting you. My purpose in this chapter is not to lay out a program for loving an addict. Instead, I hope to refocus your attention on your own heart. We will consider how your heart becomes diseased when you focus out of shame, control, or fear on the addict you love. Please read me loud and clear. I am not telling you what you should or should not do with the loved one in your life. I don't know! And if anyone promises you a program that will guarantee your loved one will stop his or her addictive behavior, you need to run from that person! Like the promises that you have heard from your addicted loved one, those promises of a "cure" for the addict will inevitably fall short.

But some promises do come true. When you relate to your loved one out of faith, hope, and love (instead of shame, control, and fear), *you* will be transformed, even if your loved one never changes. In order to move from wanting the people in our lives to change to really wanting our own transformations, we will need to let go of some big commitments:

- the determination to make things happen
- thinking, planning, obsessing about the other person because "we're only trying to help"
- forcing things to happen because we know what is best
- determining to chart a certain course because we're in the right
- maintaining control because we're afraid of what will happen if we let go
- continuing to try to save someone because we don't know what else to do
- trying to make the pain go away
- staying involved because we have to
- doing things the same way because that's the way we've always done it
- taking charge (playing God) because somebody needs to do it

THE EXODUS

The Old Testament offers a powerful lesson in how to be with people who are in bondage.

Perhaps you remember the story. The Hebrew leader Moses had been raised by foster parents. God gave him a job he didn't want or feel equipped for, because he also had a speech impediment. Sound familiar? Maybe your childhood and your credentials haven't prepared you to face the struggles in your life caused by addiction. Maybe you feel tongue-tied about telling your loved one how much his addiction has cost you and how much you want him to change. It seems like your words come out all wrong, and even when they come out right, they don't have a big impact. You don't feel like the right person to lead anyone to the promised land. In fact, you feel doomed to a land of broken promises.

That's why I like this story. Moses made some mistakes. He was over 120 years old by the time he finished this journey. His people got derailed a lot along the way. They wandered for over forty years. Only a few entered the Promised Land. Moses himself did not get to go into this longed-for new country. Doesn't sound encouraging, does it? But it is realistic. In reality, you will make mistakes and get sidetracked. For a long time, you might not see redemption in the people you love. We know the statistics. A lot of addicts don't change. You might not make it into the land overflowing with milk and honey, easy living, and wonderful relationships. But listen to the final words describing Moses: "Moses was 120 years old when he died. His eyesight was sharp; he still walked with a spring in his step. The People of Israel wept for Moses.... No prophet has risen since in Israel like Moses, *whom GOD knew face-to-face.*"[6]

Moses's life offers us a stern kind of hope. Walking alongside people who have been in bondage allows us to know God intimately. Knowing God face to face—maybe that *is* the Promised Land.

FROM SHAME TO FAITH

Research indicates that most families will suffer with an addicted family member for seven years before they will begin to tell others about this reality in their lives. When our loved ones are in the midst of unspeakable behaviors, it is all too easy to believe that they are saying something about us—our inadequacy, our failings, our unlovability.

How can you not feel ashamed when your husband drinks too much and makes a fool of himself among friends and family—again? It's hard not to believe that it's your fault if your son or daughter is struggling with an addiction. You wonder, *Where did I go wrong in parenting?* Most women who discover that their husbands are addicted to pornography live with self-reproach: "It must be something about me that makes him do this."

A poignant illustration of love mixed with addiction and shame is the movie *Leaving Las Vegas*. A woman who loves an alcoholic finds that she cannot compete with his bottle. In a moment of utter despair, she pours whiskey over herself, hoping the alcohol will allure the man she loves to a few moments of connection. He stumbles toward her, but then collapses in an alcoholic stupor. She is left in humiliating shame and loneliness.

Again, Moses's story offers hope. His leadership began in shame. God commanded Moses to go to Pharaoh, the ruler of Egypt, and tell him, "Let my people go." Moses knew that he wasn't the man for this job. Apart from wondering how in the world he would ever convince Pharaoh to do such a thing, he had a speech impediment. Some theologians believe that Moses spoke with a lisp. I picture shame enveloping Moses as he debated with God about confronting Pharaoh and leading the slaves: "They won't trust me. They won't listen to a word I say. They're going to say, 'GOD? Appear to him? Hardly!' "[7] Moses didn't trust himself, the Hebrew slaves, or God. That's what shame does. It shuts down trust. It prevents faith.

When you focus on what's wrong with you and recount all your failures with the addict that you love, there's no room for faith to grow. Our inadequacies are very real,

> The world breaks everyone and afterwards many are strong at the broken places.
>
> —ERNEST HEMINGWAY, writing to Sherwood Anderson, May 23, 1925

and the people in your life often have hurtful failures and foibles. What do we do with them?

It is possible to see the addict in your life as a means to reveal the raw parts of yourself so that they can be addressed and even healed. The wounds that you are experiencing due to your addicted friend or family member can be good news, as you learn to change *yourself,* not your friend or loved one. I know that this is a hard lesson to take in, but it is worth considering.

I remember the distraught mother who came to see me. She had discovered that her adult daughter was struggling with bulimia. The mother shook her head in despair, "I can't believe that this is happening to me." Of course, the bulimia wasn't happening to her. Her daughter was ensnared in this addiction, but perhaps there was something that could come in dealing with her daughter's struggle for this mother to learn about *herself.*

I remember the wife who shook her head in disgust when recounting her husband's addicted behavior, "I can't understand why anyone would want to do that!" I knew all too well that the stories of those addicted to substance abuse can be shocking and embarrassing. But what if there was something here for this wife to learn about her own weaknesses and need of forgiveness and grace?

When we face the painful and horrible behaviors in addiction, our first and deepest instinct is to do everything in our power to get our loved ones to change. We become desperate to make our husband be responsible, to get our son or our daughter to stop acting out, to win back our spouse from the clutches of addiction—an understandable but naive and completely dysfunctional hope. We keep hoping that our loved ones will become who they are supposed to be and stop embarrassing us and themselves. In trying to rescue our loved ones from their addictions, we become ensnared in the most insidious addiction—the last addiction, the belief that we are responsible for saving others or saving ourselves.

The power of addiction in the lives of those we love reminds us relentlessly that we need faith in a power greater than the addiction and greater than ourselves. Faith compels us to believe that God can be trusted with the people in our lives. When Moses decided to act out of faith and not shame, he asked God how he should confront Pharaoh with this invitation to set the Hebrew slaves free.

"Tell him you were sent by I AM," God said.

In the midst of our watching and waiting while our loved ones struggle with addiction, God is whispering, "I AM the One who convicts, I AM the One who changes, I AM the one who delivers." When we try to assume these roles in the lives of others, we miss our own opportunity to be convicted, changed, and delivered.

When you sense shame in the shadows—after your loved one behaves badly, or you demean yourself by trying to pacify or please someone else into changing—consider this one simple question: what does the addict's behavior show you about yourself and your own journey of change? When I feel discouraged or desperate about someone else's behavior, I think back to Moses. At first he thought God's instructions were all about the pitiable Hebrew slaves, the unreasonable Pharaoh, and his own inadequacies. He didn't know yet that God is the I AM who does many things at once. God was in the process of transforming a stammering foster child into a faith-filled prophet whose name is now synonymous with liberation: "Never since has there been anything like the signs and miracle-wonders that GOD sent [Moses] to do."[8]

When you determine to do your own work in the face of your loved one's struggle, you will need the support of others and their eyes to help you see the signs in your own life. I recommend Al-Anon, the Twelve Step group for family members of addicts. Author Frederick Buechner wrote about his experience with Twelve Step groups after struggling with his daughter's eating addiction (anorexia). These groups set him free from shame and moved him to faith:

> They also have slogans, which you can either dismiss as hopelessly simplistic or cling on to like driftwood in a stormy sea. One of them

is "Let go and let God"—which is so easy to say and for people like me so far from easy to follow. Let go of the dark, which you wrap yourself in like a straitjacket, and let in the light. Stop trying to protect, to rescue, to judge, to manage the lives…of your husband, your wife, your friends—because that is just what you are powerless to do. Remember that the lives of other people are not your business. They are their business. They are God's business because they all have God whether they use the word God or not.… It also is God's business. Leave it to God. It is an astonishing thought. It can become a life-transforming thought.[9]

FROM CONTROL TO HOPE

Our desire to control the addict can take many forms. It can be patronizing. When you find yourself lecturing or pontificating about your loved one's behavior, you are hoping to control. But judgment and lecturing never bring anyone to change. We really do become like the grownups in the *Peanuts* cartoons, with disembodied voices, transmitting sounds that register no meaning to the listener.

Control can also take the form of anger. And who can blame the loved ones of addicts for being angry? They give us plenty of cause. At the movies, we stand up and applaud when the downtrodden character finally explodes, "I'm madder than hell. And I ain't gonna take it no more!" The problem with this self-righteous expression of control is that it can actually become intoxicating. Exploding in anger or subtly maintaining an edge of contempt can feel good at the time, just like alcohol or drugs, but the consequences are harmful to your own soul and to your relationships. You never get a resolution from anger. And even though the addict's behavior is often objectionable, to scold or humiliate him is to behave violently yourself. You can certainly tell your loved one that you are angry or hurt, but when you do it in an outraged, offended energy, you just fuel the toxicity of the relationship.

Another form of control is manipulation. If you decide to hide the bills, ignore the needs of your children, or tell a "little white lie" in the hopes that you can prevent your loved one's addicted behavior, you are manipulating. And whether the manipulation is benevolent or ill intended, it is always a losing strategy. No one thrives when she is being manipulated. It may lead to a form of compliance, but it will never engender health or love. And what we truly long for in our loved ones is an attainment of the heart.

As the leader of the wandering Hebrews, Moses had to put up with a lot of grumbling and "relapsing." After God's miraculous parting of the Red Sea, the Hebrew children became afraid and wondered if it would be better to go back and be slaves again. Sounds like the addicts I have known and been! At length, Moses and his stumbling followers came to Mount Sinai. Moses climbed to the top and met God face to face. When God gave Moses the Law, Moses came back down the mountain to promise the Israelites that things would go well for them if they followed God's laws. They promised they would. Moses then went back up on the mountain for forty days and forty nights to hear further instructions.

But the Israelite people got restless, irritable, and discontented. They relapsed. They went back to their old ways and made a golden calf to worship.

When Moses returned with the first ten laws, he saw that his followers had broken their promise to worship only the God who described Himself as I AM. Moses got angry. Threw a fit. He exploded in rage. He flung down the tablets that contained the law God had spoken to him and smashed them to bits.

Moses tried lecturing, patronizing, scolding, and humiliating—and then he went back to God and complained, "Look, you tell me, 'Lead this people,' but you don't let me know whom you're going to send with me. You tell me, 'I know you well and you are special to me.' If I am so special to you, let me in on your plans."[10]

I'm glad this episode is included in the story. Once again, Moses doesn't show the certain and glowing faith that we might expect from one of the fathers of our faith, but his experience is realistic. The beginning of surrendering control is expressing our doubt.

> All religion begins with the cry "Help."
>
> —WILLIAM JAMES

In Anne Lamott's novel *Joe Jones,* Louise, who loves the addict Joe, sounds a bit like Moses. Louise anguishes over her addicted loved one and complains to God, "It's just that, as long as You're there, why don't You *act* like You're there?… You could reveal yourself. It is like, say you have a small child who wakes up from a nightmare and wanders around in the dark, calling for its parents. And the parents won't answer. They hide. The kids are having nightmares, and You hide."[11]

It is necessary to feel the pain of our confusion and our failure to control. After Moses's lament, God promises to be with him. Then Moses makes one request of God, "Please. Let me see your Glory."[12]

I think this is how Moses went from control to hope. He didn't ask for his own glory or for a glorious change in the people he led and loved. Instead, he begged to see God's glory.

And God answered, "I will make my Goodness pass right in front of you."[13]

When we focus our attention on the addict we love and on ways to solve his problems, we miss the goodness of God that passes right in front of us. No, turning to God does not mean that your life will suddenly become warm and fuzzy, or that you won't feel pain and longing for your loved one. But your focus will change. Instead of striving for control or needing the people in your life to be okay, you will surrender to wanting something (or Someone) more than you want your loved one to change.

This might seem inconceivable to you in the midst of uncontrollable and unpleasant circumstances. However, I want to suggest that evidence of God's goodness is right in front of you, *in* the heartbreak you are experiencing right now. Without the pain, you wouldn't seek Comfort. Without the confusion, you wouldn't need Wisdom. Without being lost, you wouldn't need Someone to find you. Without the utter hopelessness that you feel at times in relationship with an addict, you wouldn't need a Hope that is out of this world.

After crying out to God, Moses came down the mountain with hope—and with all of the laws carved, again, in stone. God's laws were set in stone; Moses's first hope was that he could control the unruly Israelites, and then he offered God's laws in hope that the Israelites would find God. A later rabbinic story reminds us that God continues to offer us words of hope, sometimes in the most unlikely places:

> A disciple asks the rebbe, "Why does Torah tell us to 'place these words *upon* your hearts'? Why does it not tell us to place these holy words *in* our hearts?"
>
> The rebbe answers, "It is because as we are, our hearts are closed, and we cannot place the holy words in our hearts. So we place them on top of our hearts. And there they stay until, one day, the heart breaks and the words fall in."[14]

FROM FEAR TO LOVE

Last night I went to a yoga class. I am trying something new, and I am not very good at it. I stay tense through the whole class, which kind of negates the whole point of yoga. This time, I think my instructor recognized my anxiety and wanted to help me see how it was getting in the way of my having a good yoga experience. She began the class by telling us that she was going to take note of who was not doing the poses correctly and point them out to the entire class, so that we could learn from one another's mistakes. Read that as "from *my* complete uncoordinatedness." Anyway, that's how I heard her, and so throughout the whole session, I was all worked up, fearful, tense, and dreading the moments when I would become the bad example for the class.

But the instructor never interrupted us. When class ended, she said, "Some of you were spending all your time tense, anticipating embarrassment and shame, and trying to control it and deal with it before I made an example of you. You missed the whole point of the class. You can simply acknowledge that you won't do everything the right way, and that some poses will be painful. Just wait for that to happen, and trust yourself to deal with it when it does."

She sounded so wise, and I thought to myself, *So that's what* Zen *means.*

And then I realized that her wisdom applied to loving people, especially difficult people, troubled people, addicted people. If you have been in a relationship with an addict for very long, you know that pain is inevitable. If we spend all of our time being tense, anticipating something terrible, and dreading and fearing what is to come, we miss the whole point: engaging with God in the midst of painful relationships. But waiting and trusting when chaos and confusion reign? That doesn't sound Zen, it sounds impossible.

It is important to note that behind every shadow of shame and every guise of control stands our fear: fear of embarrassment, betrayal, harm, disappointment, heartbreak. In fact, fear is a natural human response to the behaviors of addiction. There is a lot to be afraid of. But if you believe that you must ward off all pain, anticipate every move that your loved one makes, and prevent anything terrible from happening, fear will swallow you whole.

The New Testament tells us the antidote for fear: "There is no fear in love. But perfect love drives out fear."[15] Perfect love? It's hard enough to imagine loving ordinary people perfectly—but addicts? We feel the way I did in my yoga class, afraid of others, afraid of ourselves.

Loving an addict seems like an overwhelmingly complicated task because we don't understand God's love. We see God as austere, unflappable, and unmoved, a view that makes us ashamed and hopeless about our own stories and our sometimes clumsy, often desperate attempts to love others.

Moving from fear to love requires that we acknowledge and understand the truth about God and the story that we live by. Peter Van Breemen wrote, "The fact that our view of God shapes our lives to a great extent may be one of the reasons scripture ascribes such importance to seeking to know him."[16]

I want to ask, for a moment, that you set aside the idea that the story you live by is one about being an addict, an addict in recovery, or someone who loves an addict or an addict in recovery. I know that story shouts loudly and tends to drown out any other story. But I believe there is a deeper story, one of Perfect Love that will cast out all fear.

The traditional church suggests that the story we live by is that we are created to know, love, and serve God. I believe there is a deeper story, a story that those who have struggled deeply have the best chance of knowing that God yearns to love and serve *us*. This deeper story, which sets us free from fear to love and be loved, will be the focus of the next chapter.

The poet quoted in Anne Lamott's story of love and addiction said, "Yearning is blind." Certainly that is a deep human truth. That blindness leads us into the shame, controlling behaviors, and fear-filled realities that we have examined in this chapter. But what if God's yearning for us is not blind and He loves us anyway? loves us desperately?

Then the promises in the "Big Book" of Alcoholics Anonymous might be true:

> "We will be amazed before we are half way through. We are going to know a new freedom and a new happiness. We will not regret the past nor wish to shut the door on it. We will comprehend the word serenity and we will know peace.... We will suddenly realize that God is doing for us what we could not do for ourselves.
>
> Are these extravagant promises? We think not. They are being fulfilled.[17]

God's promises to Moses are being fulfilled *right now* as you consider Moses's story as a model for your own. The writer of the book of Hebrews put it this way: "Even though [Moses's life] of faith [was] exemplary, [he didn't get his] hands on what was promised. God had a better plan for us: that [his] faith and our faith would come together to make one completed whole."[18] In other words, Moses's struggle and your struggle are *intended* by God to come together to lead you to a deeper story. In the very next chapter the writer to the Hebrews explains, "Do you see what this means— all these pioneers...blazed the way [so that you would] [k]eep your eyes on *Jesus,* who both began and finished this race we're in."[19]

The deepest story promises Love. There are some promises that are not broken. Some really do come true.

10

THE DEEPEST STORY

Some of our stories describe abandonment, betrayal, and
ambivalence. We experience these losses and assaults as
orphans, strangers, and widows. Should it surprise us then,
that God wants to make himself known as the Father
who protects the orphans, as the Brother who encourages
the stranger, and as the Lover who cherishes the widow?
The Triune God who is One wants to redeem our story and
restore with his love what our story took from us.
—DAN ALLENDER, *To Be Told* [1]

There are two kinds of people—winners and losers. Inside each and
every one of you, at the very core of your being is a winner waiting
to be unleashed." These are the opening words by Rich Hoover, father and
motivational speaker, in the movie *Little Miss Sunshine*. As the movie
begins, we soon notice that everyone in this family desperately wants to be
a winner. Ten-year-old Olive Hoover has a dream of winning a beauty
pageant. Her father, Rich, has a nine-step program to help people put their
losing habits behind them and make their dreams come true.

Even Olive's awkward teenage brother, Duane, wants to be a winner.
An opening shot shows him lifting weights in front of a picture of his hero,

Nietzsche. Friedrich Nietzsche was a Prussian philosopher who died insane at the age of thirty-five. One of his most notable concepts identifies what is good as all that heightens power in a man and what is bad as all that is weak. In his 1895 book *The Antichrist,* he exhorted his followers to "pity the ineffectives."

Everyone in this entertaining film lives by the same story, which has at its deepest level the idea that we are our own creators. We make ourselves. And the goal of life is to become a winner. Pity the losers.[2]

I know this story. I started living by it when I was in the sixth grade and a participant in the Optimist Club speech contest. It was my first experience with competition. I won the first round. I won the second round. I discovered that I liked feeling like a winner. I got my picture in the local paper. My parents bragged about me to all their friends, and I had two shiny trophies on my bedroom dresser, cheering me on.

For the third round, the statewide competition, we had to travel to Albuquerque, New Mexico. As soon as I heard the other contestants speak, I knew that they were winners too. I stood with all of them at the front of the hall as the judges announced the first-, second-, and third-prize winners. When the third-place and second-place winners took their trophies, I knew that I would not be getting the grand prize award. I didn't get any award. I was a loser.

I can still recall standing there in shame. I forced a smile to my face to congratulate the other winners, but their joy was my sorrow. I think this is when I began the nervous habit of picking the skin away from my fingernails. When I finally joined my family after my defeat, the first thing my mother noticed was my bleeding nails. "You've picked down to the quick," she said. I stared at my fingers, unsure of what she meant. I later learned that the quick is the raw flesh, the living vital core of a thing. I understand now that this is what I was trying to find, a source of life in the midst of losing.

Flash forward in my story: I am an adult in the detox unit at Lutheran Hospital in Wheat Ridge, Colorado. I had tried many things to stop drinking. I had "whiteknuckled it" for a few weeks at a time. I had a read a book on breaking free of bondage. I had memorized Bible verses. I had attended one Alcoholics Anonymous meeting. But I couldn't stop drinking.

My parents had found me in my home, completely intoxicated. In shock and fear, they took me to the hospital. I smelled awful. There were unidentifiable stains on my shirt. I couldn't walk by myself to the bathroom to produce the urine sample requested by the emergency room nurse. My mom helped me into the bathroom, and her eyes stopped at my hands. I don't remember a lot about that night, but I remember her saying, "You're still picking at your nails." And I recall her explaining to the nurse, "My daughter isn't like this. She's bright and articulate." *"She isn't like this." She isn't a loser*—that's what I heard her say. But I knew she was wrong. I was a loser, and my desperation was coming through my hands, the longing, the emptiness, the thirst for a deeper story than trying so hard to win, and losing.

Two Stories

Two stories are at war in our hearts. The first is the story of victory, of independence: we can do it. We can create our lives, keep our lives, and save our lives. The second story is about defeat and dependence. We didn't make ourselves, we can't keep our lives on track, and we can't save ourselves. Each of us is highly influenced by the story that we choose to live by. Psychoanalyst Carl Jung taught that people are not shaped by laws, governments, and armies, but by myths—powerful stories. In this sense, a myth is a story with the ability to make itself real. It gives us understanding and creates meaning in our world. The story that we live by controls the meaning we see in the facts of our lives.

I have discovered, and experienced, that a person can profess to live by a certain story and yet be governed by another. For example, a person can say that she trusts God but live as if it all depended upon herself. A person can even profess believing in a Savior and yet worship at the altar of self-help. The story we live by is our true religion. The wise King Solomon explained it this way, "As [a man] thinketh in his heart, so is he."[3]

Many times since the sixth grade and since that awful night in detox, I have felt frozen between two stories that gave very different meanings to the facts that I experienced. Was I a loser, or a gainer, by these experiences?

What's the deepest story?

Looking in the Mirror

If you ask ten different addicts or their families and loved ones to write about their experiences, you will hear different stories, each linked by distinct shame-filled, unspeakable experiences. In this book I have tried to tell true stories about addiction, not shrinking back from its realities. Some of them are painful, poignant stories of loss, hope, and more loss. Some are ultimately awe-inspiring stories of courage and progress toward recovery. All are stories of desperation, stories that could be told with shoulders slumped and heads bent down. All are stories of losers.

Perhaps that last sentence made you wince. Where's the redemption in that? Maybe you want me to add that they somehow became winners through courageous effort. We don't like stories that don't have a happy ending.

Nevertheless, I believe that the deepest story beckons us to look steadily in the mirror and face our desperation, because only this truth can break us out of the story of self-effort, self-help, and self-rescuing. Facing our desperation, we can acknowledge the last addiction. Whether we say we're Christian or not, this last addiction is what isolates us from God. Blaise

Pascal wrote that understanding desperation comes from radically experiencing it. No one experiences desperation more radically than addicts or their loved ones. I have one more simple, awful story that reveals my own desperation. When my mother accompanied me to the bathroom in detox all those years ago, I was able to produce a urine sample in the plastic sample cup that the nurse provided. As we walked back to the examining room, my mom had to stop me from raising that cup up to my lips to drink from it. Shame still fills me as I recall this story. I don't tell it to be graphic or dramatic, but to say I understand desperation. I understand losing—losing self-respect, self-control, and self-help. And I have to ask what was really going on in that awful moment. Was I simply drunk out of my mind? Or was there something deep within me compelling me to acknowledge my desperate thirst and my need for a story that would quench a desire that I could not satisfy myself?

We need to look straight at our desperation and see its truth—its anguish, its activity—before we can recognize that it reflects the image of God. The most radical experience of desperation is not just part of my own story, but it reflects the deepest story—God's story.

The Hebrew word *kamar* helps express the intensity of such desperation. The verb *kamar* is defined as "to shrivel as with heat, to be deeply affected, to yearn." The word graphically suggests someone who actually loses control of his bodily functions while contemplating his desperate longing. In the hospital detox unit, I was not only under the influence of alcohol, but also under the influence of kamar. Desperation is a gift, because kamar leads us to the deepest story.

Kamar shows up in the Old Testament in the court of King Solomon. Two hysterical women stand before the king, trying to gain possession of the same baby. Both women are outcasts—losers—each with no man as her advocate. Solomon wisely calls forth the truth by asking for a sword to split the infant in two.

The king's command revealed the baby's real mother.

The woman whose son was alive was filled with kamar—"her *bowels yearned* upon her son"—and she desperately thrust her baby into the arms of a cruel stranger to save his life.[4] The story suggests a mother who lost control of her bowels while trying to save the son she loved. Her kamar revealed what was true in this confusing dilemma.

Perhaps you recognize this kamar: longing for a loved one who is in the grips of a cruel addiction, longing to escape from a torturing habit, longing for someone to choose you and rescue you from anguish, longing to be free. Addicts and those who love them suffer from ulcers, insomnia, and all manner of distress caused by kamar. I know that it is hard to believe that this desperate longing is something good. But I believe it is the prologue to the deepest story, the story whose plot is the Way, the Truth, and the Life.

Desperation hounds addicts and their loved ones, taunting us, "You are alone. You have to find your own way out of this. You can't do it. You must do it." Even those who have overcome addiction or detached themselves from the "losers" in their lives know that there are moments that catch us unaware: when you are loading the dishwasher; waiting to make a left-hand turn; reaching for the mail; or the moment just before sleep steals the day, when a vague uneasiness flits before your eyes and desperation whispers, "If you let your guard down, everyone will know that I am the secret you keep hidden even from yourself."

But kamar is not the end of the story. God does not shrink back from desperation. He weaves it throughout His narrative. Consider just the New Testament stories about the people Jesus chose to interact with: the woman caught in adultery, the prostitute humiliating herself by pouring perfume on Jesus's feet, the outcast tax collector, the pitiful man blind from birth, the thirsty Samaritan woman who could not keep a husband, the sick and grasping ragwoman, and the doubting, denying, betraying disciples. I believe God tells their stories because their desperation is a reflection of His own.

THE MIRROR HAS TWO FACES

We fear desperation, we hate being losers, because we fail to understand God's desperation. His anguish, humiliation, and relentless pursuit reveal the potential holiness of my desperation. I can accept being a loser when I understand how God wins. *He wins by losing.* The apostle Paul explains it this way: "Though he was rich, yet for your sakes he became poor, so that you through his poverty might become rich."[5] Seeing God's desperation can transform mine.

I have never told anyone this. That night when my parents delivered me to detox, when I finally made it to my room, I saw a vision. I saw Jesus. You might scoff that I was merely a drunk who was hallucinating, but I recall this image with great clarity. It was an image of light and love, a tender face with sorrow as its most distinguishing mark. I asked Him, "What are You doing here?" He answered, "*You* brought me with you." I remember pondering the next day: if that was true, then He was there when I got drunk, when I couldn't walk, when I tried to drink my own urine. At my worst, my lowest, my most helpless, He was in me. I was in Him. And that is my deepest story. It's not a story about becoming a winner but about being loved.

What does this story mean? First, that I am a loser. A loser and a failure. Second, my maker is God. And how does He make me? Not through self-assertion or self-help. He wisely and tenderly uses the gifts of addiction—getting caught, surrender, humility, woundedness, and brokenness—to make me into a woman who first and foremost knows that she is loved. The tenets of His story explain His process: that the first will be last, and the last will be first; that the meek are blessed, for they shall inherit (not conquer) the earth; that you lose your life to find it. In God's story there are not two kinds of people, just one—the lost who have been found, the losers saved by grace.

In *Little Miss Sunshine,* all the characters are trying to save themselves and end up creating their own private hells. In fact, when Duane, the teenage son, welcomes his uncle to their home, he greets him by saying, "Welcome to hell." When we live by the story of overcoming and self-help, making ourselves winners, we create our own hells. Self-help doesn't explain life. It only explains life's limitations. Self-help is not life, but the ending of life. When we come face to face with our desperation and look for a different story, we discover the truth of the New Testament:

> We…see God's original purpose in everything created. For everything, absolutely everything, above and below, visible and invisible,…*everything* got started in him and finds its purpose in him. He was there before any of it came into existence and holds it all together right up to this moment…. So spacious is he, so roomy, that everything of God finds its proper place in him without crowding. Not only that, but all the broken and dislocated pieces of the universe…get properly fixed and fit together in vibrant harmonies, all because of his death, his blood that poured down from the Cross.[6]

I can stare in the mirror and see desperation's hideous reflection, yet how sad if I cannot also see the reflection of the image of the Most Holy. Philosopher-rabbi Abraham Heschel wrote, "We discover that the self in itself is a monstrous deceit, [and] that the self is something transcendent in disguise."[7] We can value ourselves only by grasping how much God loves us. I think that is why throughout His stories God radically communicates His transcendent way of desperation—as desperate Parent, Lover, and Savior—and tells us the deepest story.

GOD AS DESPERATE PARENT

The desperation of God as parent begins in His first story, when He asks Adam His unending question to all wayward children, *"Where are you?"* It's not a simple question. Certainly God knew the precise location of the bush behind which Adam cowered. His question is the agonized cry of parents whose daughter is on the streets doing drugs or whose son spits, "I can take care of myself!" as he walks out the door: *"Where are you?"*

I have a friend whose son was on the streets for weeks in a vicious cycle of using meth and finding a way to pay for more meth. She spent the nights in her car driving up and down the streets, looking for her son. *"Where are you?"* She was filled with kamar.

Desperation in parenting does not come only in the form of parents looking for children, but in the form of children longing for parents. When we have been abandoned, abused, misunderstood, or neglected by our parents, we are strangely drawn into behaviors that guarantee a reenactment of the old, familiar struggles that we grew up with. Addicts act in ways that push others to abandon them, abuse them, and leave them misunderstood, often in a state of neglect.

Are you ready to give up on love, thinking that you love too much or need love too much? Consider one of Jesus's New Testament stories. I wonder how modern psychoanalysts would diagnose the father or the prodigal in Luke 15. It is impossible to exaggerate the desperation of the prodigal son as he ends up homeless and penniless, slopping hogs and eating scraps from the pigpen. It is equally impossible to exaggerate the father's desperation, his daily watch and wait for his wayward son. The terrible tension is finally broken. Jesus describes their reunion: "While he was still a long way off, his father saw him and was filled with compassion for him; he ran to his son, threw his arms around him and kissed him."[8]

The word "compassion" here is the Greek *splanchnon,* the equivalent to the Hebrew *kamar,* "to have the intestines yearn." Desperate loved ones of addicts need only envision the sleepless father, scandalously gathering up his robes with one hand and holding his cramping stomach with the other, running wildly to his son, to see the strange sacredness of their own desperation.

I saw the reverse of this story take place in Parker Valley Hope, a residential treatment center where I have volunteered. There I met a woman who had abandoned her children to her own alcoholism. She had hurt them and scared them. Now she found herself alone and feeling about as much like a loser as possible. She had gotten her second DUI after she passed out while driving on the interstate, running into a divider on the highway. She believed that her children would never speak to her again. She was desperate to rewrite her story of loss, abuse, and abandonment.

One afternoon, she walked out of a group meeting to find her seventeen-year-old daughter waiting for her. The girl held a bouquet of balloons, a basket of chocolate-chip cookies, and a stuffed teddy bear. The bear came from the mall's Build-A-Bear store. The daughter had implanted a sound chip in the bear, so that when the mom pressed the bear's paw, she heard her daughter's voice saying, "Nothing you can do can make me stop loving you."

Mom and daughter hugged each other. In the midst of tears and loosened balloons floating to the ceiling, I sensed *kamar,* and I saw the reflection of the Most Desperate One. In the New Testament, considering the wayward children of Jerusalem, Jesus cries out, "How often I have *longed* [this is similar to *kamar*—"to desire"] to gather your children together, as a hen gathers her chicks."[9]

GOD AS DESPERATE LOVER

Fifty million paperback romance novels are sold each year, but the love story of God makes them seem lackluster and unimaginative by comparison. God speaks to His people as a lover who has been betrayed, a lover far greater than any romantic hero. God's persistent love for His beloved is painful in its humiliating detail:

> "But you have lived as a prostitute with many lovers—
>> would you now return to me?" declares the LORD.
> "Look up to the barren heights and see.
>> Is there any place where you have not been ravished?
> By the roadside you sat waiting for lovers,
>> sat like a nomad in the desert.
> You have defiled the land
>> with your prostitution and wickedness....
> You have the brazen look of a prostitute;
>> you refuse to blush with shame."[10]

God's intention for His traitorous lover is even more staggering:

> Therefore I am now going to allure her;
>> I will lead her into the desert
>> and speak tenderly to her.[11]

God invites harlots to intimacy. It's almost beyond comprehension. He desperately hungers for intimacy—an ineffable mystery. Somehow God interacts with human stories of love sought, love lost, and love endured. The revelation of God's desperate love compels us to wrestle with the reality that He is "simply in love with us [more] than our mind is *capable* of reconciling with the way we still *have* to think of God."[12] In fact, in the Old Testament story of God's love, the beloved prostitute returns again and again to her old ways. God considers giving up on this loser who can't change her bad habits, but then with the tenderness of a lover He says: "How can I give you up...? My heart is changed within me; all my compassion [the word *kamar* again] is aroused" (translated "kindled" in the King James Version).[13]

Recently a woman came to see me for counseling, wanting help in confronting her alcoholic husband. She explained with deep remorse that she had failed to deal with his heavy drinking for more than ten years of their marriage. She knew that wise intervention should have been enacted much earlier, but now it was her only hope. Desperately she faced him with the truth. She was fortunate: her husband heard her hard words and is now in the difficult early days of sobriety. During the course of our work she began to tell stories of their chaotic, destructive life together. She shook her head with incredulity. "Why did I stay with him? I couldn't eat. I couldn't sleep. But I could not stop loving him." Her story is like God's story.

The deepest story shows us God's heart. Jesus embodies God for us. He is the Word of God. He is the touch of God. He is how God makes us, keeps us, and saves us. In Jesus's death on the cross, God's heart is crucified for the love of us. The Cross judges the wrongdoing of the world. There Grace descends into hell and leads a host of captives free—that is good news that addicts desperately need. God knew that all would disobey, fail, and lose, and He allowed it so that He might have mercy and grace upon all. That He might have *Jesus* upon all. He seeks, saves, and loves the destroyed. We are made by Him, saved by Him, set free by Him, and redeemed by Him. If you want to read where these truths are recorded in the Bible, check the endnotes for references.[14]

Knowing God as desperate lover answers the desperate longing of our hearts. No one longs for love or feels more loverless than an addict. Wanting to stay in control can keep us human beings from knowing—experiencing—God as desperate lover. As Robert Bly explained in his book *Iron John: A Book About Men,* "Some women want a passive man if they want a man at all; the church wants a tamed man—they are called priests; the university wants a domesticated man—they are called tenure-track people; the corporation wants a…sanitized, hairless, shallow man."[15] But we addicts know that we need a wild man. A man who will love us when we wander, when we drink too much, eat too much, spend too much…or try to drink our own urine. The God-man who has gone to the absolute extreme for us.

If Jesus is the heart of God, the representation of God's love for us, then He did not take all our sins on Himself so that He could command us, "Okay, now try harder. Try *harder.* Become more lovable." That's not freedom—that's the last addiction.

In *The Signature of Jesus,* Brennan Manning tells the story of a repressed nun, a woman in her midthirties who never smiled, laughed, or danced. In prayer she had a vision of a large ballroom filled with people. She explained:

> I was sitting by myself on a wooden chair, when a man approached me, took my hand, and led me onto the floor. He held me in his arms and led me in the dance.
>
> The tempo of the music increased, and we whirled faster and faster. The man's eyes never left my face. His radiant smile covered me with warmth, delight, and a sense of acceptance. Everyone else on the floor stopped dancing. They were staring at us. The beat of the music increased, and we pirouetted around the room in reckless rhythm. I glanced at his hands, and then I knew. Brilliant wounds of a battle long ago, almost like a signature carved in flesh. The

music tapered to a slow, lilting melody, and Jesus rocked me back and forth. As the dance ended, he pulled me close to him. Do you know what he whispered?... "I'm wild about you."[16]

Peter Hiett, my pastor and the one who has influenced my understanding of the gospel more than anyone else, reflected on this story of the repressed nun. He urges us, "Don't be afraid of Jesus. He's the One you long for, so wild He'll hang on a cross and sacrifice everything for you. He wants your freely given, naked heart."[17] You don't need to be afraid to commit your life to Someone who gives His life for you.

GOD AS DESPERATE SAVIOR

In his monumental book *The Crucified God,* the German theologian Jürgen Moltmann attacks the view that the crucified God is detached, unmoved: "And because he is so completely insensitive he cannot be affected or shaken by anything. He cannot weep, for he has no tears. But the one who cannot suffer cannot love either. So he is also a loveless being.... But in that case is he a God? Is he not rather a stone?"[18]

Moltmann further argues that Jesus entered the despair of Gethsemane and Calvary in order that, by acknowledging His own desperation, human beings might become more fully human. The agonizing cry of Jesus on the cross invites the release of human tears of rejection, loss, and despair. However, even Moltmann is unwilling to see God as desperate, asserting that Jesus came primarily to reveal humanity, not deity. But I am convinced that, most astoundingly, the crucified God reveals the desperation of deity.

Redemption of my own despair did not begin until I stopped reading the Bible as if it were a textbook of answers for Sunday school questions and saw this story in light of the desperation of God. Slowly, I became intrigued, even dumbfounded, by the stories of the Bible. Reading John 19,

I encountered a story of such desperation that my pink women's devotional Bible fell to the floor. I wept as I saw anew the coarse wooden cross, the gambling executioners, the crude nails, the gaping wounds, the cup of vinegar, the cry of utter despair from the fatherless Son, and the anguished turning away of the sonless Father.

I saw it clearly: God became the most hideous creature, described by Frederick Buechner as the One with the swollen lip, cauliflower ear, and ruptured spleen. In a flash of stunning light, shattering my darkness, I knew that God could look at me with kamar because He had looked away from His own Son. This was a God of desperate grace who desires all men and women to be saved.[19]

Those who live by this deepest story know that the crucified One shows the way because "he came to us not with the crushing impact of unbearable glory but in the way of weakness, vulnerability and need. Jesus was a naked, humiliated, exposed God on the cross who allowed us to get close to him."[20] At the cross, the very first became last, that we might be first. The winner became the loser, so that the losers could become winners. At the cross, Jesus revealed the glory of God—love, mercy, and unquenchable grace.

AN INVITATION TO LOSERS

Jesus has invited us to a party greater than any in our wildest imaginations. Those of us who have created our own hell know that there is no party in hell, but Jesus is hosting a party for prodigals, addicts, and losers with no requirements, no entrance fees, no credentials necessary. Does this picture of extravagant redemption scare you? We've always believed that we need to *do* something to deserve our invitation. But we're already invited, like the prodigal son. Don't be like the older brother in Jesus's story, the older brother standing in the hell of his dark field, saving himself.

How does this deepest story change anybody's personal story of addiction? That's a good question. I wish that I could tell you that there were steps to follow, principles to adhere to, and lessons to learn that would guarantee freedom from addiction. And then again, I don't. That wouldn't be true redemption; that would make it too easy for us to believe that we save ourselves. Redemption is only possible to the degree that I am lost in God's story. Reading His stories, meditating on His stories, allowing His stories to make sense of my own, I am invited to surrender to redemption. And as I surrender, I discover that I have been redeemed already.

This is the mystery of redeeming love. It allows no one to remain unchanged. The movie *Little Miss Sunshine* brings all the characters face to face with their own failures, and then they begin to love. The last one to fail is the little sister, Olive. Her goal drives the whole film: to compete in a beauty pageant to be named "Little Miss Sunshine." For the talent competition, she has learned a surprise dance. Her perverted grandpa, who died on the way to the contest, has taught innocent little Olive a striptease to the song "Superfreak." Shocked, the pageant hostess tries to stop the performance. Olive has failed.

The surprise of the story is that her father—and her brother, her uncle, and her mother—all choose to lose with Olive. They get up on the stage and dance with her.

The plot may sound silly, but this movie speaks profoundly to me of the Deepest Story. I've *been* Olive—certain I could win, only to find myself humiliated, making a fool of myself again. But God—the Father of orphans, the Brother of strangers, the Lover of widows, the Savior of sinners—chooses to lose with me. He joins me and asks me to dance with Him, and that dance is love.

I used to believe that we were all desperately searching for God, that addiction is a reflection of our search for something to fill the "God-shaped" hole inside of us (a concept Pascal originated as a "God-shaped vacuum"). But my experience of redemption in the humiliating and broken places of my story has taught me that the deepest reality is that *God is searching for us.* In the midst of our pain and foolishness, we wonder why God isn't doing anything about it. But in fact, the pain, failure, and foolishness are driving us to God. Redemption does not mean that God meets our needs and then our souls stop longing. No, redemption does not eradicate kamar. Instead, redemption allows us to surrender. We don't give up craving. We give in to craving God. And God doesn't want *something from us.* He wants *us.*

11

THE HEALING PATH

Heal me, long-expected Love; heal me that
I may continue. Renewal, release; let me begin
again without this fault that bears me down.
—THORNTON WILDER, *The Angel That Troubled the Waters*

I walked into a vast gray hall in the ruins of an ancient civilization. Broad stones stepped down to a round pool, now filled with dirt and crumbling gray rock. Near the top of the stairs, a sign read in both Hebrew and English, "And Jesus said to the man who had been ill for thirty-eight years, 'Rise, take up your pallet, and walk.' See John 5." I was standing inside the walls of the Old City of Jerusalem, at the pool at Bethesda. I knew the story from my Sunday school days. I imagined those who had once come here, the sick, blind, and malformed, lying on the steps by the pool that promised healing. I could almost hear their groans, sighs, and wails of pain and desperation. Those ruins also spoke to me of people broken by addiction and those who love them—the alcoholic, the family crippled by the lies and promises of their loved ones, the bulimic, and the man who can't stop looking at pornography.

The New Testament recounts the experience of one man among the blind, crippled, and paralyzed visitors to Bethesda. This particular man had been sick for thirty-eight years. According to John's gospel, "When Jesus saw him…and knew how long he had been there, he said, 'Do you want to get well?' "[1] The sick man answers Jesus's question with what seem to me to be excuses: "Sir, when the water is stirred, I don't have anybody to put me in the pool. By the time I get there, somebody else is already in."[2]

I know, and love, addicts and their family members who have waited for years to be healed, believing that everyone else gets the "miracle" but them. In the New Testament story, Jesus doesn't answer the man's excuses, shame him for being in this state for thirty-eight years, or even give him a shove into the "miracle pool." He simply says, "Get up, take your bedroll, start walking." John's gospel reports that the man was healed on the spot. He picked up his bedroll and walked off.[3] In his beautiful play *The Angel That Troubled the Waters*, Thornton Wilder calls this character "the mistaken invalid." "Mistaken" because his paralysis was not permanent. His condition was part of his transformation. Thornton Wilder adds these words from the healed man, "Glory be to God! I have begun again."[4]

Healing, miracles, beginning again—isn't that what we all long for? I see this story as important because it reveals how complex healing can be. Miracles often take time and are sometimes missed because we don't understand the healing path. The story suggests that Jesus took notice of this suffering man when He "knew how long he had been there." I believe coming to the pool of healing for thirty-eight years had made this man ready for Jesus.

Wilder's literary imagination offers us understanding of the implications of the gospel account. What I love about Wilder's perspective on this story is that the "mistaken invalid" knew that he needed something. He hoped it could be found in the pool at Bethesda, where he had heard others had found their miracles. In Thornton Wilder's fictionalization of this story, he includes another man at the pool who longs for healing as well. Wilder names him "the Newcomer." Unlike the man with the thirty-eight-year miracle, this man has only recently become aware that he needs healing. He doesn't look sick. He has no outward symptoms, but something has shaken his heart to bring him to this place for the desperate. To the Angel who stands by the pool, the Newcomer explains, "Surely, O, Prince, you are not deceived by my apparent wholeness. Your eyes can see the nets in which my wings are caught; the sin into which all my endeavors sink half-performed cannot be concealed from you."[5] The Newcomer's symptoms were not as obvious as the "mistaken invalid's" were, but his desperation for healing is the same.

Some of my readers are like the first man Jesus healed. You know you need healing; you need something to bring renewal and release from the burden of addiction. But I hope there are others reading too, perhaps to help a family member or loved one, who realize more subtly that you yourselves need healing also. We all do. We all get lost in our workaholism, people pleasing, and numbing behaviors as we try to escape the pain of life and the messiness of loving others. But some of us appear more whole than others, and that may be the greatest danger of all. It results in the last addiction: we rely on ourselves to heal ourselves, and so we miss the healing path.

LOOKING FOR SIGNS ON THE PATH

Every few years I run a marathon. Each one is 26.2 miles of agony and surprising joy, of physical suffering and spiritual dependence on God for something I tell myself every few miles that I certainly cannot do. I run to remind myself that I can do hard things, and that I can't, that I need to cry out to God continually, "Help!" What keeps me on the path and goads me on to finish are the signs along the way. First there are the mile markers. These are the official signs posted by the race sponsors to indicate each mile and/or kilometer along the way. I rejoice at every mile marker, and as soon as I pass one, I begin to visualize the next. Other signs keep me going too, signs held up by the cheerers-on that say, "You can do it!" "You rock!" and

"We are all Kenyans!" (That last sign refers to the amazing ability of the Kenyans to run with beauty. Seemingly effortlessly, they capture the best times and prizes in most marathons. It is an honor to even be in the same race with them! It lends me courage and hope.)

The path from addiction to healing is like a marathon in many ways. I have discovered that markers of progress on the healing path from addiction are means of encouragement as well. They have kept me going, reminding me that healing is not often instantaneous. Unlike the marathon, the healing path from addiction is not always linear. It often includes coming back for help and hope, as much a part of the miracle as any one moment of release.

Suffering

We are more likely to despair in suffering than to see it as a sign that we are on the path of healing. Many addicts in recovery make the mistake of thinking that once they drop their addictions, suffering will drop from their radar screens as well. But suffering is part of the human condition, and we cannot expect to be exempt. Most of the craziness in addiction—relapses, frenetic activity to try to save ourselves, and rage and shock at the addicts we love—comes when we run away from pain. The only thing worse than feeling pain is not feeling pain, because attempts to numb or escape pain will often lead to addictive behaviors.

We have to accept suffering, but that is not the whole story. In facing the darkness that is a part of addiction, we need to believe in the Light more than we believe in darkness. We must believe in redemption as much as we believe in the pain and heartache. Easy to say, but how do we do this? We look for redemption everywhere. Writer and recovering alcoholic Anne Lamott is brilliant at finding redemption in the midst of suffering. She calls these signs "ribbons of grace." She wrote, "Being human can be so dispiriting. It is a real stretch for me a lot of the time. I put my nose to a crack in the wall so I [can] smell the pine."[6]

The healing path has markers where sufferers can put their noses to a crack in the wall to smell grace. Sometimes that grace comes in the scent of pine or lilacs in the spring, or it may be in the laugh of a child or the melody of an old hymn. Recently my brother Jay ran the Boston Marathon (he's a far more serious runner than I am). The suffering and redemption that he found on the path were more glorious than crossing the finish line. In an e-mail to me, he described the last mile of the race:

And now, Heartbreak Hill. The center of Boston lore. Validation that if you repeat something long enough—say for 111 years—it becomes accepted as truth. Then a four-hundred-foot rise in elevation becomes "the challenge of a lifetime." On this 111th running, there was wind, 25-mph headwinds and dark, brooding skies. All the elements to depress the spirit. Questioning the hype again—suddenly, the wheelchair. His head hangs to the side. A small drool leaves his mouth. He has turned the chair backwards as he nears the crest of the Hill to avoid the risk of rolling back down. Fighting the wind, inching backwards. Lifeless legs. Indomitable spirit. Now, I feel the heartache. Often asked by others and honestly, by myself, why do you do THIS? Shouldn't you be doing something—anything else? But there on the outskirts of Boston, I cried out to God—mindful of the unbelievable blessing of an able body. Why run? How could I not accept God's gift.

A crack in the wall—Jay noticed someone else's story and got a whiff of someone else's courage to get "revenge" against Heartbreak Hill: redemption in the midst of suffering.

I found a crack in the wall myself one day while I was in Israel. We visited Yad Vashem, Israel's unforgettable memorial to the six million Jews killed in the Holocaust. The memorial includes many buildings and open spaces, with tributes to the children of the Holocaust, to the families of this terrible time in history, and to the helpers of the victims. I spent the entire time in just one exhibit entitled "Spots of Light: To Be a Woman in the Holocaust." The title reminded me of Lamott's idea of ribbons of grace. This exhibit simply featured a film with different women talking about what had helped them survive in the prison camps. The film was breathtaking in its beauty and simplicity and heartstopping as its narrators told their stories of unthinkable suffering. I took notes on the film as quickly as I could on the back of my museum map. I could not catch the names of the women speaking, but their words caught me. One woman summed up her time of torture so powerfully that I dropped my pen and paper to the floor. Her words still replay in my mind: "We all wanted revenge, and we learned that the best revenge against suffering was to try to develop a spiritual life."[7]

Tears streamed down my face at their courage. In the face of unspeakable suffering, these women looked for something More. We know that we are on the healing path, not when suffering stops, but when in the midst of suffering, we seek those things that cannot be seen. Paul says it this way in the New Testament: "So we're not giving up. How could we! Even though on the outside it often looks like things are falling apart on us, on the inside, where God is making new life, not a day goes by without his unfolding grace.... There's far more here than meets the eye. The things we see now are here today, gone tomorrow. But the things we can't see now will last forever."[8]

HUMILITY

Humility is another important sign on the road to healing. Humility affects our manner of *being* in the world rather than our manner of doing.

A gentle presence with ourselves and others is the evidence of humility. Humility frees us from embarrassment about ourselves or our loved ones and keeps us open to the healing path, in whatever form it might take. I learned my own need for humility in my failures in recovery. I hid my relapse from others for the reason often quoted in Alcoholics Anonymous meetings: "You don't want to relapse, because then you have to go to the back of the line." Right, I didn't want to go to the back of the line, and I certainly didn't want anyone to tell me that I had to go there. I had stepped off the path, not because of my relapse, but because of my pride. I was unwilling to believe that my relapse needed to happen because I still had a lot to learn. Humility allows us to hear that every relapse or struggle is an opportunity to learn something, and then humility leads us to what we need to learn, even from the back of the line.

Humility is a deep knowing in my soul that I can't do it. It is the final answer to the last addiction. One of my favorite lines in Wilder's play about the pool of Bethesda comes near the end. The Newcomer confesses that he needs to be healed, even though he looks whole.

The Angel simply replies, "I know."

Humility allows us to confess what God already knows and to hear His deep compassion and desire to be present *in* our struggles, not necessarily *over* them, or distant from them. No—He is *in* us.

As I have confessed, one of my addictions is workaholism. I often find myself pushing the needle to Full even though I am clearly on Empty. The result is an exhaustion that can lead to despair. A few weeks ago I woke up in this reality once again. I felt inadequate for the day ahead. Shame slithered in, reminding me of all my failures, and I started the day crying. Like the "mistaken invalid" by the side of the pool, I didn't think I could get up, and I was exhausted by being in this place for so many years.

Was that humility? No, not yet.

I have learned that humility becomes shame when we speak into the dark. Merely voicing our fears, failures, and distress will trap us on a dark merry-go-round that leaves us dizzy. But humility keeps us on the healing path when we speak into the light—or to the Light, the Light of the world. So I cried out, "Jesus, I don't have anything to offer to those who will come to see me today."

I heard Him—in my spirit—say, *"I know, but I will sit in the chair with you while you work."*

Then I said, "And, Jesus, I'm lonely."

And He said, *"I know. I'll be lonely with you."*

And then I said, "And, Jesus, I looked at my bank account last night, and I'm afraid about the future."

And He said, *"I know. I am your future."*

And then I said my deepest truth in that moment: "And, Jesus,…I don't trust You."

He said, *"I know."*

———

You are on the healing path when humility does not demand that God or others fix you. Instead, humility nudges you to invite the Divine Presence or the presence of others into the midst of your struggles.

OTHER-CENTEREDNESS

Beyond humility, a significant marker on the healing journey, stands the encouraging sign of focus on others. Humility allows us to invite the presence of others into our pain, and out of that comfort flows the desire to be with others in their pain. The final step of the twelve for Alcoholics Anonymous goes like this: "Having had a spiritual awakening as a result of these Steps, we tried to carry this message to alcoholics." Note that it doesn't say, "Having recovered completely..." The invitation to help others along the healing path is extended to those who are also on the path, not those who have reached some destination. Francis MacNutt, known for his teaching about healing prayer, wrote about the powerful connection between the hurting and the healer, emphasizing the spiritual principle that when we open ourselves to pain, we become part of the medicine that heals the world. MacNutt points to the experience of Michael Gaydos, "who received healing of his own impaired eyesight and became effective in healing prayer for those with a similar affliction." MacNutt wrote, "His experience leads us to an interesting conclusion: people who have been healed of a particular ailment seem to have a special gift from that point on in ministering to people with the same problem. Perhaps it is because they now have greater faith in the area in which they themselves have directly experienced God's power."[9] I think a further explanation is that the more we have suffered, the deeper our compassion runs for others who suffer. That compassion is *felt, is active* in our presence with them.

When I have the privilege to be with another addict, I experience redemption myself: release from the torture of wanting to quit drinking (or working or people pleasing); of quitting and of not being able to quit; from the merry-go-round obsession and compulsion that at times leaves me as paralyzed as the man with the thirty-eight-year miracle; from the terror of a bondage greater than myself; from the nagging sense of hypocrisy when my outside world does not match my inner world; from the guilt, shame, loneliness, and agonizing fear that I've lost the love of others or of God. Released. Redeemed.

There is a risk here, in seeking healing community or offering it, a risk of getting trapped again in the last addiction. When we believe that a "healer" has to know our pain by experience, we are vulnerable to making that person our savior or to believing that we are the savior of others. We will inevitably be disappointed by placing our faith in human healers. Disillusionment with ourselves or others can detour us from the healing path, unless we remember that there is really only one Healer—Jesus. Other-centeredness does not reveal itself only in our care for others, but also in our clinging to the One who is the most Other—the Redeemer, Jesus the Healer, embodied Love of God, who *became* our sin, woundedness, and confusion on the cross, to heal us. "God made him who had no sin to be sin for us, so that in him we might become the righteousness of God."[10] As Jesus's wounds heal us, our wounds allow us to be a healing presence in the lives of others and to believe that it is only by *His* wounds that we are healed.[11]

In his play, Thornton Wilder presents the healing of the second man, who shows signs of that healing in his care for others. First, the Newcomer complains about his healing, "I am doubly fearful that there remains a flaw in my heart. Must I drag [this]…all my days more bowed than my neighbor?" Oh, I myself have asked the same question when I have been angry and impatient about my own healing. The Angel's answer reminds me of what the healing path looks like:

> Without your wound where would your power be? It is your very
> remorse that makes your low voice tremble into the hearts of men.
> The very angels themselves cannot persuade the wretched and
> blundering children on earth as can one human being broken on
> the wheels of living. In Love's service only the wounded soldiers
> can serve.[12]

SELF-CARE

We won't stay on the path, or be able to tell that we are on it, unless we take care of ourselves. There is no all-purpose formula for self-care, however; what is nurturing and restorative for one person may not be helpful for another. For instance, Charles Dickens wrote that he walked an hour for every hour that he spent writing. I don't have enough hours in my day to follow his path, but his method does offer important guidance. Because most addicts spend many hours in introspection, we also need many hours filled with tactile pleasures like yoga, swimming, or painting.

We must care for our brains as well, since addiction often diseases the brain. Such care may mean taking an antidepressant, so that the brain can begin to circulate the natural feel-good, energizing, and relaxing chemicals that have been shut down by the addictive behaviors. It also includes what may seem like mundane living to an addict who is used to chaos—simply choosing foods with good nutrients, getting good sleep, meditating, and enjoying conversation with friends. Because the healing path often seems to take us two steps forward and then three steps back, we need to see a finished product now and then. I like to mow the lawn!

Bear in mind that we don't take care of ourselves to save ourselves. That's the last addiction. I worked with a woman who spent more time and money on self-care than most of us have: Twelve Step meetings, the acupuncturist, the chiropractor, the massage therapist, the psychiatrist, the talk therapist (me), the nutritionist, the spiritual director, and the manicurist. But she remained stuck in her addiction.

One day I said to her, "What if you stopped running from expert to expert, stayed home (or went to some quiet space), and remained quiet?" She replied immediately, "That scares the heck out of me."

"Why?" I asked. (I knew the answer though, because I too have been afraid to be with just myself.)

"I'm afraid of what I'll remember, see, and hear," she finally answered. Her answer hints at significant stories, but it is vague. She had learned to be evasive with herself and others, and as a result, she did not find true inti-macy in all of the relationships she sought and was even willing to pay for.

Addiction opens the door for us to see ourselves at our worst, so your approach to self-care depends on what you believe about sin. If you believe that sin is disgusting and reveals what is shameful and intolerable, then your self-care will be about hiding and covering up. On the other hand, if you believe that sin and the wounds it leaves are where Love gets in, then self-care can be about being merciful to yourself.

Augustine wrote, "Even from my sins, God has drawn good." If we see our addictions as the only forces that will make us acknowledge our need for God and others, then we can construct a program of self-care that springs from tenderness, rather than self-hatred.

The healing path is marked by people who care for themselves dili-gently and with compassion, because we know that One has cared for us, right in the middle of knowing everything about us. Australian theologian Kevin O'Shea wrote, "One rejoices in being unafraid to be open to the healing presence, no matter what one might be or what one might have done."[13] This openness that is essential to healing can develop only as we believe that our sin does not need to drive us from God, that when it is confessed and offered to Him for forgiveness and grace, our sin can actu-ally draw us to God. Julian of Norwich wrote of the wonder of bringing sin from the darkness into the Light: "God also showed me that sin is not shameful to man, but his glory…for…the badge of sin is changed into glory."[14] We need grace to believe that our sin can reveal our need of God, and needing Him is what He longs for us to experience. When we truly interiorize the grace and redemption of God, we become less defensive, more tender, and more free to take care of ourselves.

Anthony De Mello wrote that repentance reaches fullness when we are brought to gratitude for our sins.[15] Gratitude for my sins must include gratitude for a Love so deep that it compelled Christ to bear my sins to set me free! Gratitude for an addiction that stopped me, overwhelmed me, and humbled me becomes the means by which I can truly care for myself.

HOPE

Sometimes it's hard to see signs of hope when it comes to addiction. The statistics on rates of addiction, both in onset and recidivism, are overwhelming, and most stories tell of relapse and out-of-control and unthinkable behavior. What hope did the man have when he kept coming to the healing pool in Bethesda for thirty-eight years? I don't think he expected to encounter The Miracle. He had probably just heard stories of others who had stepped into the water and found healing. He kept coming, but ultimately it wasn't the water that healed him. It was Jesus. I think this paradox offers us the true way to understand hope.

I don't want anyone who reads this book to think I've given up on small hopes. I am not against Twelve Step groups. I attend as often as I can, and I probably need to attend more often, to be with others who remind me of the truths about addiction and redemption. I'm not against medication: I've taken antidepressants and antianxiety drugs. When my clients resisted such medications, I used to say, "What's the big deal? It is a supplement for a deficiency in brain chemistry. It's just like taking a vitamin." After I needed to get my own prescription, though, I stopped saying that. I found that it's humbling to go to a doctor and confess your unpredictable moods, paralyzing anxiety, and deep, deep sadness. I once even half-jokingly asked my psychiatrist if he could put my prescription in another name and I'd just pay out of pocket. When I handed in my prescription at the pharmacy, the clerk explained that it would be a few minutes; if I wanted to shop for a while, she would call my name over the loudspeaker when my prescription was filled. I imagined hearing "Sharon Hersh, your Prozac is ready" ringing through the aisles of the Target super-store. I told the pharmacy tech I would be happy to wait—right there, at the desk—so nobody would even speak my name. So I sympathize with the sting of using medication, even though I also endorse its value.

I'm certainly not opposed to therapy either. It's my living! The proceeds of therapy help pay for *my* therapy and prescription drugs! I consider it a privilege when people who are hungry and thirsty and naked in their souls choose to come to *me* for understanding and connection.

Twelve Step groups, medications, and therapy can be important steps along the healing path. They can even give hope a little boost now and then. *But they are not the source of hope.* I've known too many alcoholics who have relapsed because their Twelve Step groups hurt their feelings. I've known people greatly helped by medication and others who can't find the right "fit" for them and their unique brain chemistry. And I've seen and experienced how therapy can let you down, confuse you about the healing path, or even hurt you further.

There is only one Source of hope, and that is Jesus. What makes this sign of healing so hard to find is that we can't control it. Jesus doesn't use conventional methods. He does one thing for one person and doesn't do it for us. He shows up after thirty-eight years. That's why we so often return to the last addiction. It seems safer and more predictable to take matters into our own hands. We find a program, a drug, or a person that we pour all our hope into, but unfortunately there is no perfect program, medica-tion, or person.

In the New Testament story about the man by the pool in Bethesda, we learn that the healing journey wasn't simple for him either. As soon as he started telling people about his miracle, things got messy. You'd think people would celebrate his healing, but instead the religious leaders confronted him. The day Jesus healed the man happened to be the Sabbath, their sacred day. They attacked the man: "You can't carry your bedroll around. It's against the rules…. Who gave you the order to take it up and start walking?" When the healed man told them that it was Jesus, the Scriptures record, "That really set them off. The Jews were now not only out to expose him; they were out to *kill* him."[16]

Like those angry religious leaders, we really are afraid of hope, because we're afraid of Jesus. Afraid that He'll do things that don't make sense, like use broken, even faithless, people to help others. Afraid that we can't control Him and He'll break the rules, like forgive drunks, sex addicts, and moral failures. We're afraid that we are really not in control, totally dependent upon One whom we can't control.

Our resistance to hope doesn't stop God. Sometimes we need to stop all of our efforts to save ourselves, because hope breaks through when we have no other choice. We really have come to the end of ourselves. For some of us, it takes thirty-eight years or longer to hear the compassion and healing in His voice as He asks, "Are you ready to be well?" Hope starts walking without being sure where we're going. Hope keeps walking when others, or our circumstances, tell us to give up. Hope prays, "Give us this day—just today—our daily bread." Hope simply says, "I need help. I can't help myself. God, help me—in Your way." Hope doesn't hide from others when struggles resurface and doubts plague us, because now we take joy in knowing we don't have it all together, and we never will!

Hope just waits for Jesus to show up, knowing that all roads lead to Calvary. When He showed up with the thirty-eight-year miracle, His opponents wanted to kill Him, and eventually they did. When He shows up for us (and this is why we're afraid of Him), we learn that we reach life only through death. Whatever we're trusting in has to die: a career, a reputation, even a religious dogma. We become tender only when we've experienced pain. We learn that the light is our friend only when we are sick of being in the dark. Here is the hope! We really do become Easter men and women on the healing path when we surrender, give up, and die—to doing it our way, by ourselves, with ourselves.

Easter men and women participate in the dying but also in the resurrection of Jesus, a renewal and release like the man experienced by the pool of Bethesda. We will look at the concept of new life in the final chapter of this book, but we cannot separate the Resurrection from the subject of hope here.

The despair that comes when we don't include the Resurrection in our discussion of addiction has been highlighted for me as I have been watching a new reality show on television. This program, called *Intervention*, graphically chronicles the experience of an addict up to the point of an intervention, with family and friends asking the addict to get help. I watched this show for several weeks before I could identify why it often left me feeling hopeless. The show is great at re-creating the horrible world of an addict. It shows in undeniable pictures the craziness, isolation, shame, and hopelessness of addiction. As viewers watch this show, we experience the death that addiction brings to the individual, family members, and friends. And then the addict is confronted with a chance to get treatment. In the last two minutes of the sixty-minute show, we hear the addict's response to intervention (it is usually yes), and then a graphic on the screen tells where the addict will get treatment. End of show. Sometimes another graphic appears, telling viewers whether this addict is now sober or has relapsed. Frankly, in this show there are more relapses than sobriety.

Watching this program gives a compelling picture of death, with no pictures and very few words about life. As we've said, death without the Resurrection brings despair. Addiction without redemption will end in darkness and destruction. Here is the pivot point of moving beyond death, to resurrection. Easter men and women have faced their own death, have come to the end of themselves, and surrendered to Christ's death *and* resurrection. Hope springs out of new life, and new life is only possible when death gives birth to resurrection. The New Testament describes the importance of the Resurrection in finding hope: "Death swallowed by triumphant Life! Who got the last word, oh, Death? Oh, Death, who's afraid of you now? It was sin that made death so frightening and...gave [it]...its destructive power. But now in a single victorious stroke of Life, all three—sin, guilt, death— are gone, the gift of our Master, Jesus Christ. Thank God!"[17]

The Honor of the Healing Path

Suffering, humility, other-centeredness, self-care, and hope are important signs that you are on the healing path. Whether you have experienced freedom from your addiction for years, or days, or are just beginning to think that you might have a problem, the healing path is a journey of great honor. It is a journey that you can't do by yourself and that you don't have to do alone. It is a marathon race that you need to run while trusting that it has already been won. The writer to the Hebrews cheers us on:

> Keep your eyes on *Jesus*, who both began and finished this race we're in. Study how he did it. Because he never lost sight of where he was headed—that exhilarating finish in and with God—he could put up with anything along the way: cross, shame, whatever. And now he's *there*, in the place of honor, right alongside God. When you find yourselves flagging in your faith, go over that story again, item by item, that long litany of hostility he plowed through. *That* will shoot adrenaline into your souls![18]

The most recent marathon I've run was in January 2007 at Walt Disney World in Orlando, Florida. I was a bit overconfident in my training, and it showed when I began teaching a class on addiction the very next day after the marathon. I had blisters on both feet that kept me from wearing shoes while I taught! I walked tentatively and could barely move to write on the board or push buttons on my computer for my PowerPoint presentation. In that class, one of my students came to understand the healing path through my running experience. These are his words:

> When [our professor] began speaking in running language, I immediately began listening. I ran cross-country in college and had completed two marathons in my running history. I heard her words, but I did not listen to understand her. I began by listening with an arrogant heart, a hard heart, a calloused heart, a heart that would soon break. I was thinking that there was no way that [recovery from addiction] could be compared to a marathon. Equally, I thought to myself (as I had since the day that I signed up for the class) that I was not addicted to anything, but it will be good to hear about those "other people" so that I can help them in the future.
>
> I saw with my eyes the pain she was in from completing twenty-six-plus miles (because I know *that* pain) as she stood and taught me about a broken lifestyle. Moving very slowly, taking baby steps, walking up a flight of stairs in agony, not being able to bend down to pick something up off the floor—these are common the day after a marathon—I've been there, I know that type of pain.
>
> I feel as if I am at the starting line of a marathon again—my third marathon. However, this marathon will not be run with my feet—it will be run with my heart. In this marathon I won't be able to have the goal of not walking or the inner thought of just trusting in my own strength—or my own training for that matter—to just make it through it. In this marathon I am going to have to look to Someone else to run this race for me if I ever expect to make it through. I am going to have to trust in Someone else's completion

of this race if I want to take an honest look at the baggage that I am carrying in my marathon.[19]

My student grasped the essential truth. The marathon we are running is not the road to self-improvement but the path of life. The struggles along the way become the path of healing as we learn to desire a relationship with Jesus more than anything—even more than healing—and then that desire for Him *becomes* healing. After healing the man by the pool at Bethesda, Jesus commended those who have sought the healing path. May His words ring in our ears along the way: "Anyone here who believes what I am saying...and aligns himself with...me...[t]his person has taken a giant step from the world of the dead to the world of the living."[20]

12

ALL THINGS NEW

He makes all things new, so *nothing you give Him is wasted.*
You may be discouraged, tired, confused, or feeling
wretched because of sin. *Surrender* it. Give each moment
to Jesus in the obedience of faith, and that moment
becomes gold brick in the eternal city. It fits perfectly,
for it was prepared before time by God.
—PETER HIETT, *Eternity Now!*[1]

And then we went to be baptized in the Jordan River." That's my journal entry for April 19, 2007. A group from my church was touring Israel for ten days, and we'd been told that we could be baptized when we reached the Jordan River. I had never been baptized, so before the trip began, I read the account in the gospel of John about Jesus and John the Baptist:

The very next day John saw Jesus coming toward him and yelled out, "Here he is, God's Passover Lamb! He forgives the sins of the world! This is the man I've been talking about.… [M]y task has been to get Israel ready to recognize him as the God-Revealer. That is why I came here baptizing with water, giving you a good bath and scrubbing sins from your life so you can get a fresh start with God."[2]

"A fresh start." That sounded good to me. I can't think of a time in my life when those words did not entice me. We all long to begin anew—in our relationships, our parenting, our dieting, our budgeting, and even in our faith. In every experience we look for the new. At the same time we are often drawn to the old. We find comfort in those places, people, and things that we know and can count on. The old and familiar bring deep satisfaction, rest to our wandering and weary souls. Peter Hiett, senior pastor at Lookout Mountain Community Church in Golden, Colorado, was leading our Israel tour. He describes this elusive search for the new: "We all want the new and wonderful, but the older we get, the more we know that *new* gets *old*. So we get cynical. We all want the new, but we're all fearful of the new, because to get the new is to lose the old (that was new)."[3]

Those of us who have struggled with addiction especially want the new. We want to begin again, with all the shameful and shocking memories washed away, with another chance to prove ourselves and be who we know we can be, leaving the death and destruction of addiction behind.

I really thought that a dip in the Jordan River might wash away all things old and make all things new.

"And then we went to be baptized in the Jordan River." I wore my Miraclesuit, a ninety-eight-dollar swimsuit purchased from Nordstrom's before the trip. It promised to make me look like I'd lost ten pounds without even trying. Like any good addict, I was willing to buy my miracle, to pay good money for something that delivered satisfaction with no effort on my part.

At the gated entrance to the baptismal site at the Jordan River, I paid six dollars for the loan of a white robe and towel and a certificate that I could frame and display for all my friends and family to see. The entrance to the site was a bit disappointing. It looked an entrance to any commercial swimming pool that I had been to in the United States. I quickly changed into the Miraclesuit in the concrete-block locker room, put on the white robe, and walked to the river. The river's edge was a muddy stream shaded by trees, and all along its bank were sets of bleachers where tour groups could sit and prepare for their baptisms. Even though I had hoped for something more dramatic and historical feeling, I willed myself to believe that this was the place for a fresh start.

I stood back and looked at the baptismal area itself. Gates divided the Jordan by varying depths in the shallow, muddy water. The gates allowed you to choose where you entered the river, depending on whether you wanted to be sprinkled, immersed by kneeling, or completely immersed by falling backward into the murky water. I was surprised to see a lot of fish swimming around in the baptismal pool, including a twelve-inch catfish. Somehow I hadn't pictured catfish being a part of my fresh start.

Our tour guide pointed out a man standing above the bleachers at the top of the baptismal area, aiming a camera at our group. He announced that he was a photographer from Jerusalem and would take our pictures. Photos of each baptism would be available at our next hotel for four dollars each, and a video of the baptism would be ready within five minutes after the event for sixteen dollars. Photographing our memorable experience—I recalled riding the Incredible Hulk roller coaster at Universal Studios with my son, staggering off the ride with a queasy stomach, and finding a picture of the ride waiting for us at the bottom of the ramp. I bought that overpriced eight-dollar picture to remind my son of the sacrifice I'd been willing to make so that he could have 3.8 minutes of pure thrill. I wondered what my four-dollar picture at the Jordan would commemorate.

I was longing for a mystical experience, but the context was beginning to be a bit suspect—a ninety-eight dollar Miraclesuit, a six-dollar entrance fee, a twelve-inch catfish, and a theme-park photographer.

Our pastor talked to our group of approximately forty adults about water and its connection to death, surrender, and resurrection. He had several of us read out loud from the Scriptures. One passage caught me by surprise. The apostle Paul was writing to the church at Rome: "That is what happened in baptism. When we went under the water, we left the old country of sin behind; when we came up out of the water, we entered into the new country of grace—a new life in a new land!"[4]

Unexpectedly, I recalled reading that passage when I was thirteen years old, alone in my room. I'd thought about it for hours, asking God to show me what it meant, to leave behind the old for the new. Even then I was longing for newness. Now I wondered if that longing had contributed to some of the addictive patterns in my life, the desperation for all things to be new.

- A great performance brings a shiny new moment, maybe even a trophy.
- Being good and pleasing others makes you feel new, on the outside, for a while.
- Drinking makes everything new, until it makes everything so old it is unbearable.
- Working hard all the time teases with the possibility that something new is just around the corner.

Standing there by the river, I felt the desperation of this longing. Snapshots of all of the other things I had tried to find newness with came to mind—spiritual retreats, addiction treatment, and holistic health remedies. But *I* was not new. Something blocked a sustained experience of feeling new. "So then, somewhere in life we switch strategies: We give up on the new and hang onto the old. Instead of a new house, we want a home. Instead of longing for new experiences, we guard the old."[5] Family and friends of addicts often wonder why we don't give up patterns of living that are so hurtful and damaging. Why do we keep on doing the same things again and again? I think it is because we learn that we can't make things new and satisfying, and so we stick with the old, because at least it's familiar—it may be a shack of a house, but its familiarity gives us a hint of home.

I had never been baptized, because I grew up in a church that taught that water baptism was not "for us." In this present time, this "dispensation of grace," all we needed to do in order to be new was to *appropriate* Christ's death, burial, and resurrection. For many years I had tried as hard as I could to figure out what that meant. The verb *appropriate* seemed filled with effort, the very opposite of grace. It didn't seem any different than just dying, being buried, and trying to come back to life myself. Whether I *appropriated,* or died and resurrected myself, it all seemed up to me.

I've tried really hard to save myself, in all kinds of crazy ways. We all try, sometimes with religious doctrine and zeal, and sometimes with shameful addictive behavior. The alcoholic just about kills herself, then goes into a tomb until she can somehow pull herself out, and then it's new—for a while.

Even when I would count off the days of sobriety and receive the "chips" from Alcoholics Anonymous meetings commemorating thirty, sixty, ninety days of new, something still whispered and sometimes screamed in my soul, "But *I* am not new."

In my head, I understood that I am supposed to be new. I believe the teaching of the gospels, that Jesus forgives sin once and for all, gives us a clean heart and a fresh start again and again. But I did not know what to do with the restlessness in my soul that gnawed at me with a desire to *feel* new. The theology that resonated in my head sometimes didn't reach my heart, and then I *felt* the words of the apostle Paul in that letter to the church at Rome: "[I]'ve left the country where sin is sovereign,"[6] but every once in a while I go back and spend a week in our old house there.

But anyway, finally I got baptized. I didn't see the twelve-inch catfish when I was dunked. The water was cold and smelly, and the surface was slimy. I shivered, watching the rest of our group get baptized. It didn't feel mystical or magical; it felt a little silly. In fact, I was feeling thankful for my Miraclesuit that sucked in ten pounds as if they weren't even there.

ALL THINGS OLD

As I stood there, I wondered if once again nothing had really changed. I did not know yet that the surprise of newness was still unfolding. I just knew that in a few days I would return home to my whirlwind workaholic life, aching loneliness, and longing for *more*. In fact that's what the apostle Paul said in the middle of his brilliant explanation about the new life: But I need something *more*! "Is there no one who can do anything for me? Isn't that the real question?"[7] He concludes his examination of the new life by coming to the crucial conclusion that we cannot make ourselves new. He seems to understand addiction and our repeated relapses into trying to save ourselves.

As this highlight of the trip was dimming, with the realities of an experience that was more mundane than mystical and the last members of our group were being dunked in the Jordan, I felt the familiar internal clamoring of needing more. I was afraid for this experience to end with nothing significant accomplished. Even though I was in the midst of many church friends on the tour, I felt alone and let down. And then something (or Someone) arose within me to keep me on the healing path.

I whispered, "I want to go home."

Part of me did want to go home, to Colorado, where I could sleep in my own bed, find a Starbucks on every corner, and see my family and friends. But I think my whispered words were really the answer to my quest for all things new. I wanted to go home, to that place where there is the fullness of both the old and the new. The home where I will be free from suffering and struggling, and the home where I will rejoice with delight and rest in being new, without any effort of my own.

I think I was feeling homesick. Maybe that is what addiction is all about—feeling exiled from what we were made for, willing to go to desperate and destructive lengths to come home. Ask any addict, who will tell you: we are chasing a feeling, a release, a sustained comfort, a sense of ease—a coming home. Of course the home of addiction turns out to be a haunted house, full of ghosts and darkness, which only intensifies our longing for a real home. I think addicts understand best the revelations of writer and theologian G. K. Chesterton: "I had been right in feeling all things as odd, for I myself was at once worse and better than all things.... The modern philosopher had told me again and again that I was in the right place, and I had still felt depressed even in acquiescence. But I had heard that I was in the WRONG place, and my soul sang for joy, like a bird in spring. The knowledge found out and illuminated forgotten chambers in the dark house of infancy. I knew now why...I could feel homesick at home."[8]

Ultimately, the addict longs for heaven, where all things will be new and we will be home. But the addict is not willing to wait. I remember pointing this out to one of my young clients. She had just returned from inpatient treatment for her heroin addiction, and she rejected my plea that she be patient. She snapped, "Don't tell me to wait for heaven. I am only nineteen years old! I need something now." Was that just the impatient, demanding addict in her doing the talking? No, I think it was the human in her. We all long for something, *now*. Anyway, that's what I was thinking as I stood shivering on the banks of the Jordan, homesick—uneasy because I wanted all things to be new now. I didn't want to wait for heaven.

A Few Things New

I was wet, but I was also thirsty. It was hot, and though the Jordan was wet, you couldn't drink it. Right then, what I really wanted was a Diet Coke. I'd searched for one at the kibbutz where we were staying, with no success.

And there by the river, a man from our group, Carter, brought me that very thing, a Diet Coke, from the gift shop at the Jordan. I received it with relief and joy!

And then Eunice, another member of our group, bought me a copy of the ready-in-five-minutes video for sixteen dollars. I wasn't going to purchase it myself, but I received it with gratitude. Maybe playing it back would show me something in the days to come.

We waited for what seemed like hours for everyone to change, make their video purchases, and get back on the bus. I fell into a conversation with another man on the trip. We talked about our journeys of finding faith in a world that gets old. I was surprised that he remembered my speaking at our church several months back about my struggle with addiction. He asked whether my struggle was "over." It could have been a shameful moment, but I wasn't even tempted to hide. I simply said, "No. I still need God and others."

During these exchanges, giving and receiving in the midst of community, I realized that I was tasting *new*. Unexpectedly, I had received gifts from others and offered my gifts to others as well. "Whenever we receive a moment in faith instead of fear, we live in that moment. That moment is *now* and eternal and new, and that's where 'I AM' is—Emmanuel, 'God with us'—and He makes all things new."[9]

I guess that's what we get on earth—a few things new. If everything here was new all the time, we wouldn't want Home. We wouldn't need God. Just as I had wished for the baptism in the Jordan River to end my struggles, I had hoped many times previously that other good experiences would make all things new. Detox, treatment, hundreds of Alcoholics Anonymous meetings, amino acid replacement therapy, and soul care retreats—by all these experiences I had really wanted God to make a new me, so that I could work harder, impact more people, and write better books. But now I was realizing that wouldn't be a new me at all—it would be an improved version of the old me, stuck in the last addiction. The apostle Paul described his experience this way: "It happens so regularly that it's predictable. The moment I decide to do good, sin is there to trip me up. I truly delight in God's commands, but it's pretty obvious that not all of me joins in that delight. Parts of me covertly rebel, and just when I least expect it, they take charge."[10]

THE WAY TO THE NEW

The apostle Paul answers his own dilemma about where newness comes from: "The answer, thank God, is that Jesus can and does [make everything new]. He acted to set things right in this life of contradictions where I want to serve God with all my heart and mind, but am pulled by the influence of sin to do something totally different."[11] I was still asking, how does Jesus make things new in the midst of things that are old? And I am coming to understand that there is a twofold answer to this question.

First of all, He stirs our desire for home and at the same time relentlessly reminds us that we aren't there. But He promises a home ahead: "Do not let your hearts be troubled. Trust in God; trust also in me. In my Father's house are many rooms; if it were not so, I would have told you. I am going there to prepare a place for you. And if I go and prepare a place for you, I will come back and take you to be with me that you also may be where I am."[12]

Every craving for familiar addictions, every relapse, every agonizing moment over family and loved ones who are in trouble is a longing for home. Every treatment program, every holistic therapy, every counseling appointment is a revelation of a desire for *more*. And that desire can take us back into the labyrinth of addiction again and again, or it can lead us to ask, as the disciple Thomas did after Jesus promised a home, "Lord, we don't know where you are going, so how can we know the way?" Jesus said to him, "I am the way and the truth and the life. No one comes to the Father except through me."[13]

While we stay in the Way here on earth—longing for Home—the second part of experiencing the new has to do with what we do with *the* Way, the Truth, and the Life. We believe with our heads and our hearts that we are *in* Jesus—cleansed, made new, already home in His eyes. And it means that we experience Him, while we are here, in small moments made new. I thought about all those scriptures that we had read together before our baptisms and understood something new: baptism is also just a moment. It is a moment in time when we commemorate something eternal. When I surrender to the reality that what I get here on earth is moments— moments of understanding in the midst of craziness and suffering; moments of community in the midst of loneliness and isolation; moments of forgiveness in the midst of shame and struggle; and moments of hope in the midst of hard (sometimes mundane) work—then I can rest. Surrender to these moments keeps me from reaching for my addictions in anger or impatience. I'm not Home yet, but I know, heart and soul, that Home is prepared and waiting for me.

———

And so by the banks of the Jordan River, holding my Diet Coke and sixteen-dollar video, I prayed, *God, see my heart and know I long to be in the Way. That's really why I put on my Miraclesuit, handed over my six dollars for entrance, and let my pastor dunk me in the Jordan River—home to twelve-inch catfish—because I want the same thing I wanted when I was thirteen. I think I'm a little more desperate now. I want all things new. But I know that being in the Way is not an instantaneous, magical event, free of pain, sin, and struggle. I surrender, wanting to want* You *more than I want ease, accolades, relief, or achievements.*

I closed my eyes, saying this prayer on the bank of the Jordan River. All of the sounds of the vendors, my church friends on the tour, and my own internal voice quieted. I'd given up on any deep meaning for this baptism, but then it happened, my moment of mystery. I heard—I really did hear—Jesus speaking in my spirit: *Sharon, I never asked you not to drink or work or try so hard. I just miss you when you do.*

In that moment, I felt like I was home. In surrendering to Him, I discovered that He was surrendered to me. In wanting Him, I realized that He wanted me. And in missing Him, I felt the awe and wonder of hearing that He missed me.

My pastor says that trusting in the Way lets us walk in newness of life, here and now, and lets us glimpse by faith the place where everything is made new. "Whatever the case, one day a trumpet will sound, and there will be no doubt. You'll see the city of God with a new body and new eyes. And you'll say, 'This is *it*! I'm *home*!' For everything old is new, and you recognize it, for you have visited this country in faith, hope, and love. You can go home."[14]

We have considered many gifts of addiction together, the gift of getting caught, of humiliation, of surrender, of powerlessness, of forgiveness, and of hope. And as we near the end of our discussion, I suspect that while reading, you have felt a moment of conviction or relief or even a moment of frustration or impatience. As you close the pages of this book, I suspect you will experience the inevitable letdown that comes when we've encountered something (or Someone) meaningful. You may be tempted to conclude that this is yet another book that promised answers and came up short—you are still not new. I urge you to go beyond that reaction and rest in the deepest truth of this book. You cannot save yourself. But there is One who can save you. And how does He save you? This is key. He doesn't erase your problems or eradicate your suffering. He loves you.

God's love is unconditional, eternal, merciful, unchanging, vulnerable, sacrificial, and unquenchable. God's love leads us Home. The great gift of our addiction is the opportunity to know—really know—that you are desperate for Love, to give up on yourself, and to give in to Another. The personal stories in this book offer examples of how to give in to Him. If you still feel that you need a more tangible answer, or if you fear that this will all slip through your fingers during the realities of your life, I encourage you to take to heart the words of the apostle John. Let these words become your home when you are tempted to wander, or when you get lost again along the way: "What marvelous love the Father has extended to us! Just look at it—we're called children of God! That's who we really are."[15] Don't stop looking for or looking at His love. Giving in to Him is the last answer to the last addiction.

I've had a longtime friend who had been in recovery for over thirty years. Everyone in our Twelve Step group loved to hear his stories of experience, faith, and hope about addiction. Two years ago, he was diagnosed with lung and liver cancer. At a Twelve Step meeting, someone asked him if he was tempted to go back to alcohol, since his days were numbered. He replied, "No. That's not the way that I want to go home." His confidence in the face of death reminded me of the words of Eusebius, an early father of the church: "He needs not fear confiscation, who has nothing to lose; nor banishment, to whom heaven is his country; nor torments when his body can be destroyed at one blow; nor death, which is the only way to set him at liberty from sin and sorrow."[16]

I went to visit my friend in the hospice, knowing his time was short. Later I learned it was the day before he died. While I sat by his bedside, he drifted in and out of awareness. At one point he opened his eyes, looked straight at me with light filling his face, and said, "Tell them—tell everyone—that it's real."

And so I'm ending this book telling you that the Love and the Home that we all long for are real. The *More* we long for is real—more real than anything that we experience in this life. We get tastes of *More* when we surrender to waiting for the day when we are really home and all things are new. Waiting is hard: scary, risky, humbling, maybe embarrassing. We have days of great joy and days of great struggle. We rely on ourselves and remember that we need God. We live like exiles and find others to walk with us along the Way. We are enticed by the promises of this world and long for the promises of a world to come. We take two steps forward and three steps back. But if we will just give in and be quiet for a few minutes, we can hear God's whisper: *This is how I am making all things new.*

NOTES

Introduction

1. Gerald May, *Addiction and Grace* (New York: HarperCollins, 1988), 43.

2. William Cope Moyers, *Broken* (New York: Viking Penguin, 2006), 3–4.

3. See Acts 17:28, NIV.

4. Benedicta Ward, ed., *The Desert Christian: The Sayings of the Desert Fathers* (New York: Macmillan, 1980), 64.

5. 1 John 3:20.

6. 1 John 3:20.

7. Julian of Norwich, *Julian of Norwich: Showings,* trans. Edmund Colledge, OSA, and James Walsh, SJ (New York: Paulist Press, 1978), 338–339.

Chapter 1

1. Linda Schierse Leonard, *Witness to the Fire: Creativity and the Veil of Addiction* (Boston: Shambhala, 1989), xv.

2. Lee Reinsch, "Man Says He's Addicted to Cable; Wants to Sue Charter," *Fond Du Lac (WI) Reporter,* January 7, 2004, 1.

3. Bob Dylan, "Gotta Serve Somebody," *Slow Train Coming,* Columbia Records, 1979.

4. See www.robertperkinson.com. Also see www.family-drug-intervention.net, "Every family in America is somehow affected by drug addiction and alcoholism" (accessed 10/18/2007).

5. Matthew 6:21, NIV.

6. 2 Corinthians 5:5, 2.

7. As quoted by Dominic Maruca, "A Reflection on Guilt," *Human Development* 3:1 (Spring 1982): 42.

8. Anne Lamott, *Traveling Mercies* (New York: Anchor Books, 1999), 184–87.

9. Dan Allender, PhD (lecture in sexual disorders class, Colorado Christian University, Lakewood, CO, Spring 1994).

10. Walter Brueggemann, *Awed to Heaven, Rooted in Earth* (Minneapolis: Fortress, 2003), 116.

Chapter 2

1. Bernice Kanner, *Are You Normal?* (New York: St. Martin's, 1995), 98.

2. Kanner, *Are You Normal?* 113.

3. Lecture on public speaking, The Leadership Institute, Greenville, SC, April 2004.

4. From John 8:1–11. I also tell this story in my book *Bravehearts: Unlocking the Courage to Love with Abandon* (Colorado Springs, CO: WaterBrook, 2000), 127–28.

5. Marnie C. Ferree, *No Stones: Women Redeemed from Sexual Shame* (New York: Xulon, 2002), 17.

6. Marion Woodman, *Addiction to Perfection* (Toronto: Inner City, 1982), 13.

7. Psalm 63:1, NIV.

8. Alcoholism/Drug Abuse/Teen/www.robertperkinson.com.

9. Mark 16:15, NIV.

10. As quoted by Mother Teresa, "I Thirst for You," in *Bread and Wine: Readings for Lent and Easter* (Maryknoll, NY: Plough, 2003), 34.

11. Thomas Merton, *Contemplative Prayer* (London: Darton, Longman and Todd Ltd, 2005), 78

12. Richard J. Foster, *Celebration of Discipline: The Path to Spiritual Growth* (San Francisco: HarperSanFrancisco, 1998), 123.

Chapter 3

1. Abby Ellin, "Addicted to Work? Sure, Isn't Everyone?", *New York Times,* August 18, 2003, 1.

2. Diane Fassel, *Working Ourselves to Death: The High Cost of Workaholism and the Rewards of Recovery* (Lincoln, NE: iUniverse, 2000), np.

3. Mark 8:36–37.

4. Genesis 3:5, NIV.

5. Jack London, *John Barleycorn* (Santa Cruz, CA: Western Tanager, 1981), 5–6.

6. Luke 18:10–13.

7. Martin Buber, *I and Thou* (New York: Continuum, 2004), 81.

8. Deuteronomy 8:3, NIV.

9. Margaret Bullitt-Jonas, *Holy Hunger: A Woman's Journey from Food Addiction to Spiritual Fulfillment* (New York: Vintage, 1998), 70.

10. Proverbs 29:18, KJV.

11. Quoted in Ernest Kurtz and Katherine Ketcham, *The Spirituality of Imperfection: Storytelling and the Search for Meaning* (New York: Bantam, 1992), 152–53.

12. William H. Crisman, MDiv, STM, *The Opposite of Everything Is True: Reflections on Denial in Alcoholic Families* (New York: William Morrow, 1991), 24.

13. Kurtz and Ketcham, *The Spirituality of Imperfection,* 164.

14. William James, *The Varieties of Religious Experience* (1902; repr., New York: Mentor–New American Library, 1958), 98–99.

Chapter 4

1. Michael E. Zimmerman, *Eclipse of the Self* (Athens, OH: Ohio University, 1981), 247.

2. Luke 11:35–36.

3. C. J. Swett and M. Halpert, "High Rates of Alcohol Use and History of Physical and Sexual Abuse," *American Drug and Alcohol Abuse* 20 (1994): 263–72.

4. Dana Candler, *Deep unto Deep* (Kansas City, MO: Forerunner, 2004), 4.

5. Benedicta Ward, trans., *The Sayings of the Desert Fathers: The Alphabetical Collection* (Kalamazoo, MI: Cistercian, 1975), 167.

6. Galatians 2:16, 19; 5:23; 3:22.

7. Isaiah 53:2–6.

8. Brennan Manning, *The Signature of Jesus* (Sisters, OR: Multnomah, 1988), 220–21, quoting Thomas Merton, *New Seeds of Contemplations* (New York: New Directions, 1961), 35.

9. Quoted in John Garvey, *The Prematurely Saved and Other Varieties of Religious Experience* (Springfield, IL: Templegate, 1986), 15.

10. From *Bread and Wine: Readings for Lent and Easter* (Maryknoll, NY: Plough, 2003), 1.

Chapter 5

1. Henri J. M. Nouwen, *The Wounded Healer: Ministry in Contemporary Society* (New York: Bantam Doubleday Dell, 1979), 88.

2. Luke 3:8–9.

3. Susan Cheever, *Note Found in a Bottle* (New York: Washington Square, 1999), 188.

4. St. Frances de Sales in a letter to Madame de la Flechere, dated May 1608, quoted in "The Little Virtues," published by The Monastery of the Visitation, St. Louis, MO.

5. 2 Corinthians 4:6; 1 Corinthians 1:27, NASB; 2 Corinthians 4:7, NASB.

6. Luke 23:34, KJV.

7. Gerald May, *Addiction and Grace* (New York: HarperCollins, 1988), 139.

8. William Silkworth, *Alcoholics Anonymous: The Story of How Many Thousands of Men and Women Have Recovered from Alcoholism,* 3rd ed. (New York: Alcoholics Anonymous World Services, 1976), 58.

9. Romans 1:23.

10. Rilke is quoted by Margaret Miles, "Pilgrimage as Metaphor in a Nuclear Age," *Theology Today* 45:2 (December 1988): 174.

Chapter 6

1. Peter Hiett, "Sex Appeal" (sermon, Lookout Mountain Community Church, Golden, CO, October 4, 2004).

2. Patrick Carnes, *Don't Call It Love: Recovery from Sexual Addiction* (New York: Bantam, 1992), 22.

3. Rev. Michael J. Cusick, MA, LPC, founder/director, Restoring the Soul, Lakewood, Colorado, www.restoringthesoul.com.

4. Jennifer Schneider, MD, PhD, and Robert Weiss, MSW, CAS, *Cybersex Exposed* (Center City, MN: Hazelden, 2001), 24–25.

5. Steve Siler and John Mandeville, "Traitor," *Somebody's Daughter*, copyright © 2005, Nashville, TN: Music for the Soul. Used by permission.

6. Leonard Shengold, MD, *Soul Murder: The Effects of Childhood Abuse and Deprivation* (New York: Ballantine, 1989), 6.

7. A. A. Milne and Ernest H. Shepard, *The Complete Tales of Winnie-the-Pooh* (New York: Dutton Juvenile, 2001), 187.

8. 2 Peter 3:8, NIV.

9. Romans 4:17, NKJV.

10. Dana Candler, *Deep unto Deep* (Kansas City, MO: Forerunner, 2004), 11.

Chapter 7

1. Caroline Knapp, *Appetites: Why Women Want* (New York: Counterpoint, 2003), 53.

2. Quoted in "The Lean Years," *Elle*, March 2007, 425.

3. Caroline Knapp, *Drinking: A Love Story* (New York: Dial, 1996), 8.

4. Professor Al Andrews, "Psychopathology," Colorado Christian University, Lakewood, CO, Fall 1996.

5. Wendell Berry, "Song in a Year of Catastrophe," *The Selected Poems of Wendell Berry* (Washington DC: Counterpoint, 1998), 76.

6. Joe McQ, *The Steps We Took* (Little Rock, AR: August House, 1990), 23.

7. Sterling Thomas, *Sacred Hearts: Daily Reflections for Divine Renegades* (Denver, CO: Quantum Mind, 2000), 61.

8. Margaret Bullitt-Jonas, *Holy Hunger: A Woman's Journey from Food Addiction to Spiritual Fulfillment* (New York: Vintage Books, 1998), 241.

9. Quoted by Simon Tugwell, *Ways of Imperfection* (Springfield, IL: Templegate, 1985), 229.

10. Romans 2:4.

11. Brennan Manning, *The Wisdom of Tenderness* (San Francisco: HarperSanFrancisco, 2002), 8.

12. Anne Lamott, *Plan B: Further Thoughts on Faith* (New York: Riverhead, 2005), 29.

13. Julia Cameron, *The Artist's Way* (New York: Tarcher, 2002), 40.

Chapter 8

1. Anthony De Mello, *Wellsprings* (New York: Doubleday, 1986), 227.

2. Silkworth, *Alcoholics Anonymous*, xxvii.

3. Kurt Cobain, *Journals* (New York: Riverhead, 2003), 3.

4. Luke 18:17.

5. Pedro Arrupe, *Hearts on Fire: Praying with Jesuits,* ed. Michael G. Harter (Chicago: Loyola, 2005), 66.

6. Psalm 42:1, KJV.

7. Ram Dass and Paul Gorman, *How Can I Help? Stories on Reflection and Service* (New York: Knopf, 1985), 51–54.

8. John 4:24.

9. John 19:28, NIV.

10. See John 1:29 and Revelation 13:8.

11. Acts 17:24–27, Barclay.

Chapter 9

1. Anne Lamott, *Joe Jones* (New York: Shoemaker and Hoard, 1985), 14–15.

2. Melody Beattie, *Playing It by Heart: Taking Care of Yourself No Matter What* (Center City, MN: Hazelden, 1999), 129–30.

3. Lamott, *Joe Jones,* 12.

4 Beattie, *Playing It by Heart,* 18.

5 Beattie, *Playing It by Heart,* 17.

6. Deuteronomy 34:7–8.

7. Exodus 4:1.

8. Deuteronomy 34:10–11.

9. Frederick Buechner, *Telling Secrets* (San Francisco: Harper, 1991), 92.

10. Exodus 33:12–13.

11. Lamott, *Joe Jones,* 55.

12. Exodus 33:18.

13 Exodus 33:19.

14. Told by William Cope Moyers, *Broken* (New York: Viking, 2006), preface from "The Politics of the Brokenhearted" by Parker J. Palmer.

15. 1 John 4:18, NIV.

16. Peter Van Breemen, *Certain as the Dawn* (Denville, NJ: Dimension, 1980), 13.

17. Silkworth, *Alcoholics Anonymous,* 84.

18. Hebrews 11:39–40.

19. Hebrews 12:1–2.

Chapter 10

1. Dan Allender, *To Be Told* (Colorado Springs, CO: WaterBrook, 2005), 181.

2. Connecting this film to the gospel and many of the ideas in this chapter come from a sermon by Peter Hiett, "The Deepest Story: Darwinism and the Seventh Day" (sermon, Lookout Mountain Community Church, Golden, CO, February 17, 2007).

3. Proverbs 23:7, KJV.

4. See 1 Kings 3:16–27, KJV.

5. 2 Corinthians 8:9, NIV.

6. Colossians 1:15–17, 19–20.

7. Abraham Heschel, *Man Is Not Alone: A Philosophy of Religion* (New York: Harper and Row, 1951), 47.

8. Luke 15:20, NIV.

9. Matthew 23:37, NIV.

10. Jeremiah 3:1–3, NIV.

11. Hosea 2:14, NIV.

12. Sebastian Moore, *The Crucified Jesus Is No Stranger* (New York: Seabury, 1977), 49.

13. Hosea 11:8, NIV.

14. Luke 19:10; John 1:1; Romans 5:19; 2 Corinthians 5:21; Ephesians 2:8–9; 4:8.

15. Robert Bly, *Iron John: A Book About Men* (New York: Vintage: 1992), 61.

16. Brennan Manning, *The Signature of Jesus* (Sisters, OR: Multnomah, 1988), 214.

17. Peter Hiett, "The Wild Man" (sermon, Lookout Mountain Community Church, Golden, CO, October 20, 2002).

18. Jürgen Moltmann, *The Crucified God* (London: SCM, 1974), 35.

19. See 1 Timothy 2:4.

20. Brennan Manning, *A Stranger to Self-Hatred* (Denville, NY: Dimension, 1982), 123.

Chapter 11

1. John 5:6.

2. John 5:7.

3. John 5:8–9.

4. Thornton Wilder, *The Angel That Troubled the Waters* (New York: Coward-McCann, 1928), 149.

5. Wilder, *The Angel That Troubled the Waters*, 148.

6. Anne Lamott, *Grace (Eventually)* (New York: Riverhead, 2007), 22.

7. Yehudit Inbar, interview from "Spots of Light: To Be a Woman in the Holocaust," Yad Vashem Holocaust Museum, Jerusalem, 2006.

8. 2 Corinthians 4:16, 18.

9. As told by Brennan Manning, *The Wisdom of Tenderness* (San Francisco: HarperSanFrancisco, 2002), 49.

10. 2 Corinthians 5:21, NIV.

11. See Isaiah 53:5.

12. Wilder, *The Angel That Troubled the Waters*, 149.

13. Kevin O'Shea, *The Way of Tenderness* (New York: Paulist, 1978), quoted by Brennan Manning, *The Wisdom of Tenderness*, 33.

14. Julian of Norwich, *All Shall Be Well: Daily Readings from Julian of Norwich*, ed. Sheila Upjohn (Harrisburg, PA: Morehouse, 1992), 142.

15. Anthony De Mello, *Awareness* (Grand Rapids, MI: Zondervan, 1997), 118.

16. John 5:10, 12, 18.

17. 1 Corinthians 15:54–57.

18. Hebrews 12:2–3.

19. Used by permission.

20. John 5:24.

Chapter 12

1. Peter Hiett, *Eternity Now!* (Nashville: Integrity, 2003), 251.

2. John 1:29–31.

3. Hiett, *Eternity Now!* 247.

4. Romans 6:3.

5. Hiett, *Eternity Now!* 248.

6. Romans 6:1.

7. Romans 7:24.

8. G. K. Chesterton, *Orthodoxy* (New York: BiblioBazaar, 2007), 79.

9. Hiett, *Eternity Now!* 253.

10. Romans 7:21–23.

11. Romans 7:25.

12. John 14:1–3, NIV.

13. See John 14:5–6, NIV.

14. Hiett, *Eternity Now!* 253.

15. 1 John 3:1.

16. Eusebius to Emperor Valens, fourth century, quoted in Peter Hiett, "Are We There Yet?" (sermon, Lookout Mountain Community Church, Golden, CO, April 28, 2007).

ACKNOWLEDGMENTS

I am profoundly grateful to…

My daughter, Kristin—your resilience and grace continue to reshape your own brokenness and the brokenness of others.

My son, Graham—your questions remind me that real faith asks, confronts, seeks, and doubts.

My parents—your courage to begin again, believe again, and try again teaches me to hope.

My friends—Clint and Jen, Joan, Mark, Judy N., Judy B., Sheri, Jenna, John, Lis and Perry. Your gentle presence in my life during the past year has been a treasured gift.

David, my wonderful counselor—your presence in my life has made His Presence more real.

Aram Haroutunian—your shepherd's heart has found me on more than one occasion.

Peter Hiett, my pastor—your courage and passion to proclaim the radical Love of God relentlessly leads me back to the story that is deeper, higher, and wider than any human story.

Dan Allender, my first teacher about addiction—your own brokenness is more beautiful than all of your brilliance.

Dudley Delffs for believing and championing this project.

Phyllis Klein, my editor, for refining ideas and raising necessary questions.

All at Waterbrook Press for allowing me to tell the stories of addicts and those who love them as well as The Story of the One who loves them most.

ABOUT THE AUTHOR

Sharon Hersh is a licensed professional counselor and the director of Women's Recovery & Renewal, a ministry of counseling, retreat, and support services for struggling women. She is an adjunct professor in Addictions Counseling at Reformed Theological Seminary, Mars Hills Graduate School, and Colorado Christian University. She is the author of several books, including *Bravehearts*, *"Mom, I Feel Fat!"* *"Mom, I Hate My Life!"* and *"Mom, Sex Is No Big Deal!"* She is a sought-after speaker for conferences and retreats. Sharon lives with her family in Lone Tree, Colorado.

Also available from Sharon Hersh

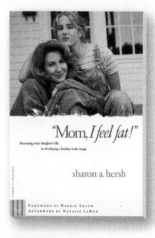

"Mom, *I feel fat!*"

Becoming your daughter's ally
in developing a healthy body image

sharon a. hersh

FOREWORD BY DEBBIE SMITH
AFTERWORD BY NATALIE LABUR

"Mom, *I hate my life!*"

Becoming your daughter's ally through the
emotional ups and downs of adolescence

sharon a. hersh

"Sharon Hersh lives and writes with brilliance, wisdom, and winsome wit. This book will allow you to examine the depth of your daughter's adolescent confidence and joy."
—DAN ALLENDER, author of the Children Series

"Mom, *everyone else does!*"

Becoming your daughter's ally in responding
to peer pressure to drink, smoke, and use drugs

sharon a. hersh

FOREWORD BY NANCY RUE

"Mom, *sex is NO big deal!*"

Becoming your daughter's ally
in developing a healthy sexual identity

sharon a. hersh

FOREWORD BY SHANNON ETHRIDGE
BEST-SELLING AUTHOR OF *Every Woman's Battle*

Navigating an adolescent daughter's emotional life is one of your toughest challenges as a mom. The Hand-in-Hand series gives you the information and strategies you need to help your daughter survive and thrive during the most vulnerable time of her life.

You know you can't have it all. Still, you want something more. Discover how your deepest longings can lead you to a life filled with rich relationships and extravagant love.

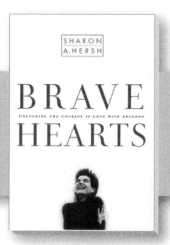

SHARON
A. HERSH

BRAVE
UNLOCKING THE COURAGE *to* LOVE WITH ABANDON
HEARTS